Sowing Seeds

Writing
for the
Christian Children's Market

Kathleen M. Muldoon
Foreword by Sally Stuart

Honeycomb Writers Press
Hemingway, SC, USA

Copyright © 2010 Kathleen M. Muldoon, © 2015 Honeycomb Adventures Press, LLC
ISBN: 978-0-9836808-4-0
Cover image © Rick Carlson – Fotolia.com; republished & repurchased: © 2015 by Lushpix Illustration

Unless otherwise noted, Scripture passages used throughout this text have been taken from the Authorized King James Version, Philadelphia, The National Bible Press.

All rights reserved. This book may not be reproduced in whole or in any form, or by any means, without written permission from the publisher.

Honeycomb Writers Press is an imprint of Honeycomb Adventures Press, LLC, PO Box 1215, Hemingway, SC 29554.
www.honeycombadventurespress.com

Originally published by E & E Publishing, Sausalito, California. Republished by permission.

Publisher's Cataloging-In-Publication Data
(Prepared by The Donohue Group, Inc.)

Muldoon, Kathleen M.

  Sowing seeds : writing for the Christian children's market / by Kathleen M. Muldoon ; foreword by Sally Stuart.

     pages ; cm

  Originally published: Sausalito, Calif. : E & E Publishing, c2010.

  Includes bibliographical references and index.
  ISBN: 978-0-9836808-4-0

  1. Christian literature for children--Authorship--Handbooks, manuals, etc. 2. Children's literature--Authorship--Handbooks, manuals, etc. 3. Christian literature for children--Technique--Handbooks, manuals, etc. 4. Children's literature--Technique--Handbooks, manuals, etc. 5. Christian literature for children--Publishing--Handbooks, manuals, etc. 6. Children's literature--Publishing--Handbooks, manuals, etc. I. Stuart, Sally E. II. Title.

PN147.5 .M85 2015
808/.06/8

Praise for Sowing Seeds

This book is amazing! I wish I had had it 15 years ago. Anyone who wants to write for children needs to read this book and keep it at his fingertips while writing! Kathleen covers all aspects of writing in great detail, yet entertains the reader with personal stories that provide practical application. I highly recommend this wonderful book for all writers of children's literature. I cannot say enough good things about it! —Crystal Bowman, best-selling author of over 70 children's books including *My Read and Rhyme Bible Storybook*.

Kathleen Muldoon says that Christian writing should "encourage, inform, entertain, and inspire." *Sowing Seeds: Writing for the Christian Children's Market* certainly fulfills all of those promises as she draws on twenty-five years of experience as a professional writer and writing instructor. Her skill at research, spinning anecdotes from her own and others' experiences, and knowledge of her subject matter makes this an indispensable book for anyone who dreams of writing for children. —Christine Kohler, author of *Words Alive! Christian Writers' Skills & Prompts*

Sowing Seeds: Writing for the Christian Children's Market will do for children's writers what *The Little Handbook to Perfecting the Art of Christian Writing* has done for Christian writers in the adult market. In practical (and sometimes humorous) ways, Kathleen covers the process of writing for this specialized market—from setting up your writing space to finding a home for your manuscript in the marketplace. I wish I'd had such a book when beginning my own writing career! —Kristi Holl has authored 35 books and has taught children's writing for 27 years.

The conversational tone and encouraging voice in Kathleen M. Muldoon's book, *Sowing Seeds: Writing for the Christian Children's Market* help give writers confidence that they, too, can experience success in this niche market. With Scriptures to encourage the writer's soul, short writing exercises to apply what's been taught, and clear explanations of the unique nuances found in this market, *Sowing Seeds* provides gentle guidance for writers hoping to experience success in the Christian children's market. —Nancy I. Sanders, author of *Yes! You Can Write Children's Books, Get Them Published, and Build a Successful Writing Career*

Practical, comprehensive, and engaging—*Sowing Seeds* is a valuable resource for writers. Kathleen Muldoon's love of authors and children shines on every page. —John Evans, author of *How to Study the Bible: A Discussion and Workbook in 12 Lessons*

In *Sowing Seeds*, Kathleen Muldoon offers writers well-researched, insightful, and clear advice on how to break into Christian fiction for children. All writers who need an easy-to-follow, step-by-step guide to writing and publishing in this much coveted market will find this resource a must-have. —Lisa Angelettie, Publisher of LisaAngelettieBlog.com

Sowing Seeds opens doors for both new writers and parents looking for that special book that will one day reach their child. It is only through God's writers that we can teach his children best, and Kathy Muldoon is an example of that type of servant. —Jessica Adriel, *Hawke's Tale* Author and Book Coach

Kathleen Muldoon's words of wisdom, as welcome showers on thirsty soil, will nudge the sprouting ideas of Christian writers toward fruitfulness as they employ her down-to-earth tools and bask in the sunshine of her encouragement. —Etta G. Martin, Editor, *Partners,* Christian Light Publications

Dedication

For Diane Gonzalez Bertrand, Lupe Ruiz Flores, Katy Jones, and Judy Woller, cherished writing colleagues and sisters in Christ.

Acknowledgments

I so appreciate being given the opportunity to write this book. I pray that it will convince Christians blessed with the gift of writing to hone those talents into a ministry of writing for Christian children.

I thank my editor, Eve Heidi Bine-Stock, for encouraging me to write *Sowing Seeds...* and for her help during the writing process.

I also thank the talented professionals who added their wisdom and experience for sections of this book: Etta G. Martin, Editor, *Partners* magazine; authors Crystal Bowman, John Evans, and Eve Christensen; Jo Louis, Editor, Little Lauren Books; and Sally E. Stuart, Editor, *Christian Writers' Market Guide*, who graciously took time from her ministry to write a foreword for this book.

Contents

Foreword by Sally E. Stuart........................11

Introduction...13

Chapter 1: *Know Thy Audience*..................17

Chapter 2: *Know Thy Markets*....................29

Chapter 3: *In the Beginning*........................43

Chapter 4: *Christian Children's Magazines—
A Treasury of Opportunity*....................55

Chapter 5: *The Joy of Short Fiction*............65

Chapter 6: *The Challenge—and Blessings—
of Nonfiction* 83

Chapter 7: *Christian Children's Books—
Storehouses of Faith Seeds*..................105

Chapter 8: *Sowing Truth Seeds through
Fiction Books*......................................115

Chapter 9: *Christian Children's Nonfiction Books—Fertile Ground*..........137

Chapter 10: *Sealed with a Prayer—Sending Off Your Manuscripts*..........167

Chapter 11: *Blessed Are They Who Wait on the Lord—and on Publishers*..........187

Chapter 12: *Giving Back*..........201

Appendix A: *Reference Resources for Christian Children's Writers*..........209

Appendix B: *Professional and Educational Resources for Christian Writers of Children's Literature*..........211

Appendix C: *Recommended Reading by Age Group*..........215

Bibliography..........221

Index..........225

About the Author..........231

Foreword by Sally E. Stuart

When I started writing over 40 years ago, much of my writing was for children. I wrote for children's take-home papers, magazines, curricula, and even did a children's picture book. Unfortunately I had little help to lead me along that path to publication. And although I sell books for writers on my Website today, I have never been able to find a how-to book for those writing Christian materials for children—until now.

I couldn't have been happier when I first saw the manuscript for *Sowing Seeds*. Here at last was a comprehensive manual for those wanting to sow those very important seeds into the lives of children. I especially like the fact that it does not just dwell on children's picture books, but covers the vast array of opportunities for children's writers. Opportunities that many writers tend to overlook as they seek a publisher for their children's material.

Many writers tend to think that writing for children is somehow easier than writing other types of material. This book reinforces the truth of the matter—writing for children is often the hardest but most rewarding of writing endeavors. The good news is that Kathleen Muldoon understands how to do it—and most important—is able to teach you how to effectively break into this field. She also understands not just the how-to of the writing, but the spiritual ramifications of what you might write for children.

When I teach writing for children, one of the most important things I try to convey is that you don't write for children as one group, but must recognize and target specific age groups. This book will help you look carefully at those age divisions, how each age group learns, and how to target the specific needs of each age level.

Sowing Seeds is even more helpful in that it includes exercises to help you put what you are learning into practice. We all learn by doing, so if you are faithful to follow through on those exercises, you will come away better understanding how to write to make an impact on these precious young lives.

As I have read this book, one of my first thoughts was that it covered all the aspects of writing for children that I would have included if I had written this book myself—but perhaps did it even better than I could have. My thought now is that I can hardly wait for it to be released so I can add it to my online bookstore. I know it's a how-to book many of my customers have been looking for.

Sally E. Stuart, *Christian Writer's Market Guide*
stuartcwmg@aol.com
www.stuartmarket.com
www.stuartmarket.blogspot.com

*Remember that the person who plants few
seeds will have a small crop; the one
who plants many seeds will have a large crop.*

—2 Cor. 9:6 (TEV)

Introduction

Jesus loved children. Whenever I read a gospel account of Jesus with a child (for example, Matt. 18:2-3), I see an image of Him wrapping an arm around that little one and exchanging endearing looks with him or her. Whenever I write for Christian children, I get a similar image of loving parents reading my book or story to their sons and daughters, and that makes my heart sing.

Because you are reading this book, I assume that you too have felt leanings toward writing for the Christian children's market. God has blessed you with writing talent, and you would like to use that talent to sow faith seeds. What better place to start than with children who are just beginning or have taken their first faltering steps on their own faith journeys? Or what of the special ministry to teens who may be at a crossroads in their faith lives? Writing for Christian children covers the gamut of ages, from cradle to college-bound. What a vast mission field for Christian writers!

Sowing Seeds

By the time I retired from my work as a staff writer for a faith-based newspaper, I felt ready to embark on a more focused direction in my freelance writing career. Theretofore, I'd written largely in the educational market, specifically hi/lo books, both fiction and nonfiction, aimed at "reluctant readers." I'd also written in the adult inspirational market. But after my first year teaching in my church's youth program, I decided to take on the challenge of writing fiction and nonfiction specifically targeted at Christian children. I soon discovered that this was my calling, both in the magazine and book arenas. I hope by the time you finish this book that you too will embrace the ministry of writing stories, articles, and books for this highly specialized market.

Christian children's literature can be found in the same outlets as all children's literature, from traditional print media, including magazines and books, to the emerging world of electronic publications. It also has its additional markets, such as Sunday school and youth program papers and newsletters. The added ingredient in these offerings is, of course, the faith element. Including Christian values and, sometimes, instruction, becomes the challenge for writers. It requires that we are firmly rooted in our own Christian lives; we can't share with readers what we don't have ourselves.

Introduction

This book is not intended to teach you how to write, since I assume that you already are a skilled wordsmith who wants to focus your talent on writing for Christian children. If you feel a need to dust off your basic writing skills—including those pesky grammar issues, I suggest you first avail yourself of a refresher course such as those you can find online. Some suggestions for these are included in Appendix B. A good grammar or style book can also help.

As we explore the various types of writing in this specialized ministry, I will suggest some polishing and style hints. Unless otherwise noted, the material contained in this book is based on my own experience as a writing instructor and as a freelance writer for the past 25 years, and it is intended to introduce you to the fertile mission field of writing for the Christian children's market. Throughout this book, the general term "children" also includes teens.

In the first couple of chapters, we will discuss my "two great commandments" of writing for Christian children: Know thy audience; know thy markets.

Chapter 3 will get you started with materials, workspace, and essential resources.

Chapters 4 through 6 focus on writing for the Christian children's magazine market.

Chapters 7 through 9 cover writing for the Christian children's book market.

Chapters 10 and 11 deal with the nuts and bolts of submitting your work and possible outcomes, including contracts (hooray!) or the dreaded "rejects" (boo hiss!).

We will also discuss the rapidly expanding opportunities in the self-publishing world and how, in some cases, Christian writers are finding this a viable alternative.

We finish with ways you should consider giving back some of your time and talents. Each chapter includes a writing exercise designed to stoke your faith and creativity.

So, are you ready? Then dig out your notebook, sharpen your pencil, and crank up your computer; we'll begin by studying the first great commandment.

Train up a child in the way he should go: and when he is old, he will not depart from it.

—Prov. 22:6

Chapter 1

Know Thy Audience

Do you ever wonder what children believe about God and Jesus? Years ago, I remember reading Eric Marshall and Stuart Hample's delightful book, *Children's Letters to God*. Some entries were poignant, some funny, and others amazingly insightful. I wondered if the letters were real or concocted by the clever authors. So when I began teaching children's church within my faith community, I asked my 5- and 6-year-old students to write letters to Jesus, telling or asking him anything they wished.

After reading their letters, I was convinced: children have definite ideas about God, Jesus, heaven and angels, and these are as diverse as their personalities, family backgrounds, and levels of understanding.

My favorite letter came from a 6-year-old (I've added punctuation and spruced up the spelling): "Dear Jesus, When I get to heaven, will Mary be my mother? Will my real mommy still be my mother too? Does Mary order you around? I hope not. I don't think I'd like heaven if there are too many rules. But I want to be with you so I guess I will try. Your friend, Graciela."

Writing for children is a privilege. Writing for Christian children is also a ministry. If you remember nothing else from this chapter, remember this: respect your audience. On my desk is a glass paperweight encasing this quote from Russian dramatist Maxim Gorky: "You must write for children in the same way as you do for adults, only better." That advice guides me as I write for this special audience, and it also speaks to those who think that writing for children is "easy." Not! Those of you who have already tried your hand at writing children's literature know that it can be the most challenging task you'll ever undertake. In my opinion, it is also the most rewarding. Being able to share my faith with children seems like (pardon the cliché) "the cherry on top" of my writing life.

One of the first decisions you will make before embarking on a writing project for the children's Christian market is the age group it will target. While these may vary a year or two depending on a publisher's guidelines, we'll discuss them in the most widely-used categories.

As we examine the level of understanding and usual interests of each age group, we'll also look at their spiritual growth. Many studies have been conducted on this subject. I like the writ-

Chapter 1: *Know Thy Audience*

ings of Judy Bryson, President and CEO of Pioneer Clubs, a ministry that is focused on small groups of children based on age; the information included on spiritual growth contains some of Bryson's observations.

Know Your Readers' Ages

There are four major age groupings to which to target your writing, as explained below:

Preschool (approximately 2-to-5 years)

By and large, these children are "listeners" rather than readers, although certainly some children are learning to read at younger ages. Parents, grandparents, and other adults buy preschoolers' reading material and are usually the readers to them.

These children are in the process of exploring and absorbing the world around them. Their five senses are particularly sharp, and writers need to remember this by including sensory details when writing for them.

Preschoolers have a sense of awe that is inspiring. Everything is interesting to them if presented in a lively, entertaining manner. These kids emulate the important adults in their lives. They also have short attention spans, and it is up to writers to bear this in mind and realize that every word must "count" and advance the story they are telling. Preschool books and magazines must compete with the high energy, flashy world of electronic media.

It is important for those writing for preschoolers to not "talk down" to these little ones. Writing on complex topics is especially challenging; the final piece must be an intriguing distillation, presented clearly and concisely. But because preschool material is read by an adult, you can include challenge words if you've made them understandable in context. For example, a board book might begin, "In ancient times there lived a man named Noah. He was a good man. And because Noah was so good, God assigned him a very special mission." Even though older beginning readers might stumble over such sentences, they are easily understood by young listeners.

Preschoolers' worlds are usually limited to home, church, family, friends, daily activities, pets, and perhaps outside experiences such as daycare or preschool, mothers' day out, and "mommy and me" type activities such as exercise and play classes, story time at the library, trips to the grocery store, and so forth. They like to see themselves in the stories they hear.

Given good parental teaching, as well as church and Sunday school attendance, preschoolers have their own conception of God and

Chapter 1: *Know Thy Audience*

Jesus. We writers must anticipate and respect these. Preschoolers know that heaven is a special place. They know they can't see God or Jesus or angels but they will draw you a picture of any of these figures if you ask. Some of these may be based on the Sunday school sheets they color. They extrapolate from these and put Jesus in a modern context. While I taught my students the gospel account of Jesus calling Peter and Andrew as disciples (Matt. 4:18-19), they were coloring a picture of Jesus on the shore, reaching out to the brothers. All three men wore sandals.

"What kind of shoes are they wearing?" I asked.

The children responded as one voice. "Flip-flops!"

According to Bryson, children up to five years old "mimic" faith. They imitate the faith they see lived out at home. Bible stories retold at a preschool understanding are enjoyed by these youngsters, especially those that involve baby Jesus, animals, and children.

Primary Grade/Beginner Readers (approximately 6-to-9 years)

Do you remember your very first day of school, that feeling of being a "big" girl or boy, but perhaps secretly harboring some fears? This experience is largely true for most children in kindergarten through third grades. They are eager, energetic, and immensely curious.

As they proceed toward those middle grade years, they also begin to question things they previously accepted as true. Learning to read opens heretofore unknown worlds to these children and also increases their sense of independence.

They develop likes and dislikes, often becoming passionate about a particular topic, such as "dinosaurs." Social skills take a giant leap forward during these years, too. Primary graders learn to form friendships and vie for their place in the family and in their world.

This is my favorite age group for which to write. To me, these children are like butterflies that have learned to spread their wings, step out of their boundaries, and see what lies beyond.

Bryson states that, for the most part, primary graders "experience faith" as their family does, although they become more inquisitive and more innovative in their own fledgling Christianity.

In some denominations, such as Roman Catholic, by the time children reach 8 or 9 they are further invested in their faith by being introduced to the sacraments of penance and Holy Communion or other rites. They begin to examine the consequences of their actions and

Chapter 1: *Know Thy Audience*

their impact not only on others and themselves but on their relationship with God.

In Sunday school, primary graders learn to pray and to understand what it means to be "good" because believers are commanded in Scripture to lead holy lives. Some of these children are introduced to the Ten Commandments. Often children in this age group are presented with their first Bibles.

Middle Graders/Intermediate Readers/ Tweens (approximately 9-to-13 years)

This is my second favorite age group—but it may become your first! As much as parents dislike this thought, it is during these years that children begin drawing a teeny bit farther away from family and gravitating more to friends (usually of the same gender).

I don't have children of my own, but I'm surrounded by them both in my work and in my neighborhood. It's been a real "trip" watching my next door neighbor Carly grow from a toddler to a confident young adult. But I most remember her middle-grade years. She was, as her mother quipped, "10 going on 40." As is typical for that age, Carly thought herself quite grown up the moment she hit "double digits." She shunned the scooters and skates she'd adored the day before. She became practically inseparable from her friend across the street, often causing her conflict at home as she tried to balance peer pressure and her family values and morals.

School is a focal point for these children, where again they must manage their academics versus "temptations" of peers, competing activities, and family obligations. Often kids in middle grades become active in sports or begin pursuing a passion such as music or dance lessons. Being a member of a group is important, as it implies acceptance.

Since friendships are so important to these children, youth groups and church attendance are particularly important. Scriptural teaching has more impact on them as they deepen their understanding that they have a responsibility as Christians. They begin to see a correlation between their actions and the privileges and degree of freedom they're allowed as a result of their choices.

Prayer is important to middle graders; this is the time when they begin to understand how and why to pray. Some may see God and Jesus as more distant as they grow, and they realize that they have to do their part to keep communications open. They usually are more realistic in their beliefs and no longer see God as a "Santa Claus" in the sky.

Many denominations have special rites for middle-grade children—such as confirmation or baptism—which make them feel more a part of their faith communities.

Teens/Young Adult Readers (13-to-18 years)

In my opinion, this is the most challenging age group for writers. Perhaps this is because so many teens consider adults to be "know nothings," as my friend's 14-year-old son told her recently. So why should they believe or care about anything we write?

When I think back to my high school years, I cringe and wonder how I ever made it through without my grandmother (who raised me) strangling me. I'm sure many of you can tell horror stories about yourselves, too. This is a time of separation and rebellion, of turmoil, change, and questioning everything from the meaning of life to the existence of God.

This is, of course, a generalization. There are those precious teens who positively bloom during this phase of their lives. Often they are the ones who have developed a close relationship with Jesus Christ and, according to Bryson, have formed their own inner value systems. These are the teens you'll find building houses for Habitat for Humanity during summer vacation, or mentoring younger children after school.

Whether teens are sailing rough seas or experiencing smooth sailing, many are searching and questioning the faith of their families. Once these teens reach age eighteen and are considered young adults, some decide to leave their faith communities. They can no longer be "dragged" to church. Others go off to college and "lose" their faith as they're barraged with secular anti-God, anti-Christian teachings. Teenagers indeed reach a crossroads in their faith as they approach adulthood. In the last three lines of his poem "The Road Not Taken," Robert Frost says it all:

> *Two roads diverged in a wood, and I—*
> *I took the one less traveled by,*
> *And that has made all the difference.*

<u>Surround Yourself with Children</u>

If you don't have children or grandchildren, if you're seldom in contact with children in your neighborhood or through your work or at church, you will find it difficult to write for this audience. You need to see and hear children, know what makes them laugh, what makes them cry, what captures their attention. Where are they in their faith journeys? You need to listen to them.

Chapter 1: *Know Thy Audience*

I'm sure the youth director at your church would be delighted to have you on board, teaching or assisting a teacher at church school or Sunday school. If you want to write for teens, perhaps you can facilitate a Bible study or arrange to mentor a high school student. With your creative spirit, I'm sure you can come up with other ways to immerse yourself in the delightful world of kids!

Ten "Rules" for Knowing Your Audience

Regardless of which of these age groups of emergent Christians you will target, it is important that you bear in mind some basic "rules" in your quest to know your audience, those whom you are targeting with your writing. These include:

1. Respect your readers.

2. Never talk down to your readers.

3. Be aware of the level of understanding and faith of your readers.

4. Do not preach.

5. Remember what it felt like to be a child during each phase of your development.

6. Bear in mind that as a writer for Christian children, your own love and understanding of Jesus and faith matters must shine through your work.

7. Your writing should encourage.

8. Your writing should inform.

9. Your writing should entertain.

10. Your writing should inspire.

Before you move on to the second great commandment of writing for the Christian children's market, Know Thy Markets, try your hand at the following exercise:

> ## Writing Exercise
> Write a paragraph or two detailing your reasons for wanting to write for Christian children.

*That our sons may be as plants
grown up in their youth;
that our daughters may be as corner stones,
polished after the similitude of a palace.*

—Ps.144:12

Chapter 2
Know Thy Markets

Recently, an editor friend and I met for lunch. We whined, as friends do, about our various life stressors—mine, the ups and downs of freelance writing, hers, an ongoing frustration *with* freelance writers. The children's magazine she edits clearly states in its writers' guidelines, "We do not accept fiction." Yet 90% of manuscripts she receives each day are fiction. "Don't writers know how to read?" she asked as we washed down our apple pie with fat-free lattes.

Studying markets, a student informed me, is an "unmitigated pain." I think most of my students and many writers would agree with that sentiment. Yet, second only to writing talent, knowing which markets might welcome your manuscripts is the road to a successful writing career. It's not enough to write the great American novel and then send it out randomly to 75 publishers hoping that one will be savvy enough to sit down and write you a six figure advance. I am convinced that I sold my first children's book manuscript and my first story for a children's magazine only because I spent hours searching and studying the markets.

You can take the pain out of knowing the Christian children's market if you approach it with prayer and thanksgiving that you have the opportunity to minister through the written word. Start now, even if you haven't yet begun to write your first manuscript for Christian children.

Let's take a look at what I consider to be the three keys to the successful launch of your writing career: reading, studying guidelines, and analyzing targeted publications.

Read, Read, Read

I thought it was a given that writers read—until I began teaching adults how to write for children. With their first assignment, my students are asked for information on their reading habits, such as which periodicals and newspapers they read on a regular basis, favorite authors, and titles of the last few books read. I actually had one student admit, "I sometimes read a magazine when I'm flying somewhere for my job. I don't read books." Others have confessed to "rarely" reading a book. Wow! That seems

Chapter 2: Know Thy Markets

incomprehensible to me. So in my never-to-be-humble opinion, your first step to a successful freelance career writing for Christian children is to read widely in the wonderful world of their literature.

What should you read? If you don't have an idea yet of what you want to write, reading everything from Sunday school papers to Christian children's magazines to Christian children's books will be your starting place. You should, during this process, come up with some ideas for your own writing.

Perhaps you'll see some cool Bible quizzes in a magazine and would like to try your hand at constructing one. Jot that idea down in your notebook.

You may read a teen book on how to keep one's faith while attending classes in a secular university. That might spawn an idea for a teen book with a different focus.

Do you or your children or students read a magazine for which you would like to write? Make note of its title; likewise, write down the names of book publishers whose styles and books particularly speak to your heart and spirit.

If you already know that you would like to write in a particular genre or market, immerse yourself in that special genre. For example, let's say you would like to write Bible stories for preschoolers, particularly board books. Read every Bible-based board book you can get your hands on.

Perhaps you'd like to write feature articles for Christian teens. Read oodles of them!

Subconsciously, you will begin to absorb the tone, style, and spirit of Christian children's literature.

So, do you have to take out a small business loan to purchase all these books and magazines? No! Start with your own church—does it have a library? What about a youth minister? He or she is sure to have a supply of children's publications you can borrow. You might be surprised how many resources you'll find within your faith community. Christian bookstores, of course, will allow you to browse, although certainly they are not "libraries." Still, at least you can get an idea of style and content just by seeing the variety of material available.

One of my favorite places to hunt is in thrift shops, especially those run by faith-based ministries. In my neighborhood, there are two terrific second-hand stores, one run by Lutheran volunteers, the other by a Catholic church. I can almost always find back copies of some of the more popular Christian children's magazines (usually at a dime apiece!), as well as Christian children's books, for which I pay about a quarter. When I'm finished with them, I donate them to my own church library.

Chapter 2: *Know Thy Markets*

Public libraries have a smattering of Christian children's books, particularly classics such as C.S. Lewis' *Chronicles of Narnia* series.

Stores that buy and sell books such as Half-Price Books also have a selection of Christian children's books. Many Christian children's magazines will send you sample copies for free or for postage only (more about this below).

And, of course, Amazon.com and Abebooks.com will link you with sellers of used books if you know the title of a book you'd like to purchase.

All right! Hopefully you already have in mind a starting place to begin growing your ministry to Christian children. Let's turn now to ways to search in depth those magazine and/or book publishers that you'd like to target.

Adhering to Publishers' Guidelines

A few years ago during a critique session of a local writers' group, a participant finished reading a lengthy "short" story for 8-to-12-year-old readers and said she planned to submit it to *Highlights for Children*.

"How long is your manuscript?" I asked. "*Highlights* has an upper word limit of 800."

"It's 1,300 words," she admitted. "But I can't cut anything without losing the story. I think they'll see that when they read my manuscript."

Not! I don't know whether or not that writer sent her manuscript to *Highlights*; I do know that if she did, it was rejected without being read. (And just as a postscript, we can almost always cut our word counts drastically without "losing" the story!)

Magazine and book publishers issue writers' guidelines for a reason, and the length requirements are often based on space constraints.

Most Christian children's magazine guidelines include the following information for writers: an overview of the publication's mission; denominational information, if appropriate; age and gender (if appropriate) of readership; genres they accept (for example, fiction, nonfiction, devotionals, activities, crafts, etc.); word limits/length—often this is different for fiction and nonfiction, and that is indicated; manuscript submission information; and the publisher's estimated response time to submissions. There is also information on how to obtain a sample copy of the magazine.

Other guideline information for Christian children's magazines might include more details about the audience (perhaps a publication

Chapter 2: *Know Thy Markets*

targets African-American children or rural children).

If a magazine is "themed," meaning all the stories and articles in an issue will revolve around a predetermined theme—"honesty," for example, writers are directed to download a list of those themes, which will also contain deadline dates for submissions.

It is important to read ALL the guidelines, because they specify information that is essential for prospective writers to know. For example, *Pockets*, a magazine published by Upper Room ministries, offers prospective writers very specific information in its online guidelines, including the fact that it is an interdenominational magazine that expects its stories and articles to reflect the multicultural and ethnic heritage of its readers. Their guidelines also remind writers that not all children live in "traditional" families and that they can live in the city, the country, or the suburbs. In other words, we writers must bear in mind the diversity of our audience and reflect such diversity in our writing.

Book publishers that include Christian children's books in their lists or that only publish Christian children's books issue guidelines that address most of the same issues as do magazine guidelines.

In addition, they also contain specific information on types of books they publish (for example, board books, comic books, chapter books, novels, etc.). Many guidelines list a few of their latest releases and also give statistics about their recently published authors (for example, 10 percent from unpublished writers, 40 percent from submissions through agents...). You can also learn whether you can submit your manuscript directly to the publisher or if you need to have an agent. Information is usually listed about how you can obtain or access a publisher's catalog, which is essential because it will show you what that house has already published.

Again, you need to thoroughly read all guideline information, because it is here that publishers tell you what they need and want—and sometimes what they don't want. For example, if you access online guidelines for Pauline Kids, the children's division of Pauline Books and Media, you'll find explicitly stated a number of genres which they do not publish, myths and romances among them. Writers submitting, say, teen romances to this publisher would waste their time and the publisher's, and would also gain a reputation of being "unprofessional" in the process.

Finally (do I hear a "hooray!"?), you are probably wondering where you can find these guidelines. For the Christian children's market, I strongly recommend your investing in the annual market directory compiled by Sally E. Stuart, *Christian Writers Market Guide*. It is

Chapter 2: *Know Thy Markets*

available for purchase online or in some major bookstores. This will be your starting place: it gives Christian publishers' guidelines for everything from greeting cards to magazines to books to Bible curricula.

I say this is your starting place because while Ms. Stuart makes every effort to have the most up-to-date information, the publishing market is fluid. Publishers cease publication and new ones spring up, sometimes daily. So after you have identified a market of interest, go online and verify the guidelines. Often you will find updated information that is vital for you to know before you submit your manuscript. For example, an editor might have a notice posted that they have put a temporary moratorium on accepting manuscripts. Save your time and postage!

Hopefully by now you have an idea of a Christian children's story, article, or book you would like to begin, and you've found a market you would most likely target first. Let's take a hypothetical journey through the final "key," analyzing your market.

Analyzing Your Targeted Market

Your reading has inspired you to write a story about a boy faced with a common dilemma:

should he cheat on the spelling test for which he has not studied? You've read a sample copy of *Pockets* and think your story might be a good fit for that market. You've read its guidelines and have discovered that the magazine has an issue coming up next summer with the theme of "honesty." You know from the guidelines that this magazine targets 8-to-12-year-old readers, that it accepts fiction, and that you are allowed a word length of 600-1000 words for fiction.

You can, at this point, write your story and send it off. But I like to take a final step before I write for a market, particularly one to which I've never submitted a manuscript. I analyze that sample copy that I simply read before. This might seem like "overkill"; however, it wasn't until I took this step that I sold my first magazine story. Here's what I look for in my analysis:

- How many fiction stories does the magazine contain? How many feature articles? How many departments / columns / features are staff-written? (You can find the names of editors and staff writers in the magazine's masthead.)

- How much space, if any, is dedicated to advertising?

Chapter 2: *Know Thy Markets*

- In contemporary stories, how much "religion" is included? How about Scripture, reference to church or Sunday school? Is the moral message of fiction stories explicit or implied?

- Are the magazine's nonfiction articles written by clergy/theologians? Is there any biographical information given on article/story authors? (This may be included in a brief sentence or two at the end of the piece.)

- What is the overall "tone" of the magazine? Light-hearted? Solemn? Inspirational?

Sometimes after I have analyzed a magazine, I change my mind about what I might submit. If, for instance, a magazine has one fiction story and fourteen articles, I may decide I have a better chance at sending nonfiction, and I conceive of a way to turn my plot idea into a nonfiction topic. Using our "to cheat or not to cheat" plot, I might instead research the problem of cheating in schools and come up with an article on this topic, such as "what would you do?" I'd perhaps then ask a dozen or so kids what they would do if they saw their best friend cheating on a test. Such an article could go in lots of different directions, use Scripture, and be written in the "tone" of the targeted magazine.

This final step in analyzing a market might sound strange but, believe me, it is helpful. I actually type a story or article—depending on which I will write—into my word processing program from my targeted magazine. Then I run the spelling/grammar review in it, paying particular attention to the readability, Flesch-Kincaid level.

When I stated above that I am convinced this depth of analysis helped me make my first magazine sale, I thought back to a terrific kids' magazine, *My Friend*, which unfortunately ceased publication in 2009. Over the first few years of my fledgling writing career, I had submitted several fiction stories to them; all were rejected. Then I hit on the idea of typing out one of their stories; just typing it told me that, first, my stories had a lot more narrative and a lot less dialogue than did their stories. Mine had less action and less humor. The average reading level of the stories I typed out was 4.1 (fourth grade, first month reading level). Mine were closer to 6.7. So I revised one of my stories, used a lot less narrative and replaced it with strong dialogue that carried much of the plot, added humor and simplified my sentence structure. That story, which had been rejected three years earlier, now sold.

Chapter 2: *Know Thy Markets*

This type of analysis works well for the book market, too. Type out a chapter or two from a book from your targeted publisher's list. You can run a similar analysis. While you're at it, note the number of pages, number of chapters, and so forth of that book, which should be for the same age group and of the same genre as the book you plan on writing.

So there you have it: reading, guidelines, analyzing—your keys to knowing your markets. Are you wondering why this information is presented here rather than toward the end of this book? It is because whether to first target a market and then write or write and then target a market is one of those "which came first, the chicken or the egg" type questions. It is probably one of the most frequently-asked questions by my writing students. And my answer is justifiably vague—do whichever works for you. As for me, I almost always write with a specific market in mind.

Hopefully, you're ready to forge ahead and do what you've been hankering to do...write. Before we get into the specifics of the many opportunities in the Christian children's market, and how you might make your writing rise to the top of an editor's slush pile, let's pause for just a moment and talk about where and when you might write. We'll do that in Chapter 3.

But first, here's an exercise for you:

> ## Writing Exercise
>
> Read and analyze a Christian children's magazine, Sunday school paper, or book. Write a paragraph or two on your overall impressions of this publication. How would you describe its "tone"—for example, casual, kid-friendly, spiritual, literary? Would your current writing style be a good fit for this publication?

Whosoever therefore shall humble himself as this little child, the same is greatest in the kingdom of heaven. And whoso shall receive one such little child in my name receiveth me.

—Matt. 18:4-5

Chapter 3

In the Beginning...

The book I most re-read while growing up is Louisa May Alcott's *Little Women*. This semi-autobiographical novel chronicled the lives of the four March sisters growing up during mid-19th century America. Despite the fact that I read this book from my favorite reading spot, the fire escape of our inner city tenement building, I still fancied myself as Jo, the second oldest of the sisters and an aspiring writer. Her need for private space in their cozy Concord, Massachusetts, home resonated with me. Whenever inspiration struck, Jo headed for the only place she could have some private writing time—a cubby she'd carved out for herself in the dusty attic.

Writing is a solitary, personal activity that requires a special place. Before you begin writing, determine where you will write. Before you crunch numbers to see if you can afford to rent an office somewhere, let me describe my "office" space.

I do not own a home nor do I rent an apartment. For the past 16 years, I have rented a single room in a friend's two-bedroom, one-bath house. That room (one of the two bedrooms) is about 10' x 10', and it suits me just fine. My friend allows me the run of the house for cooking, bathing, and entertainment. But my rented space is where I live and work. My writing nook is the 4' x 4' northwest corner of my room. I've set up a computer hutch in that corner, next to a window on the right that looks out onto our street and neighborhood. On the left of the hutch is my dresser, on top of which sits my printer and a three drawer Rubbermaid "thingy" that holds printing paper and envelopes. Going clockwise around the room from my computer hutch, on the other side of the window are two bookcases which form an "L" in the northeast corner, my twin-sized bed, a nightstand, a two-drawer file cabinet, my clothes closet, a chest of drawers, the door to my room, and a small roll-top desk which abuts the dresser. Oh, and on the carpet beneath the window is a cat bed meant to sleep one large, literary feline named Walter. Of course, Walter much prefers stretching out on the bottom of my bed, from which he can jump into my lap while I'm writing.

Chapter 3: *In the Beginning...*

I tell you all this because I want you to know that no matter what your circumstances, you should be able to find a cubby, however small, that will be used for only one thing—writing. One of my colleagues, a prolific author and mother of four, has her space atop a card table in the laundry room. Any place will do it if affords you some privacy, comfort, and quiet.

A final note—after you begin earning money from your writing, you can only claim office space as a business expense if you use a room solely for the purpose of writing. There are books written on tax law for writers; in the IRS form1040 instruction booklet, you can also find details on which such deductions are and are not allowed.

Accessorizing

Whether you have a tiny space or an entire room, your writing place should be comfortable and speak to your individuality.

We all find inspiration differently. Some of my writing colleagues find that peaceful landscapes hung near their computers inspire them to new heights. I have a simple silver cross hanging over my printer. Beside that is a small bulletin board with a calendar, a photo of Walter and another of me and my critique group

Sowing Seeds

enjoying lunch, and a few funny, writing-related cartoons.

In her writing blog, author Lisa Angelettie lists as a "must" for her writing space scented candles, a big plant, and photos of her family. (I like the idea of plants, but since I kill every plant I touch, I think it would be too depressing to have a dead plant on my dresser).

Basic Necessities of the Writing Life

A poet friend of mine insists he can only write if he uses his ancient Remington typewriter which is missing the "Q" and "Z" and for which he has to order ribbons from a catalog-based business in Vermont. I have to admit that the metal relic looks cool and "artsy" on the battered typing stand in his writing loft.

However, today's publishing market is making the need for a computer with word processing software ever more essential. E-zines and e-books are upon us, whether we like it or not.

Many publishers are now requesting only email queries—many even email submissions. On the positive side, electronic submissions bring much faster responses and save postage.

Those writers who are computer-phobic, however, are having a hard time putting away

Chapter 3: *In the Beginning...*

their portables and taking tentative steps into the world of word processing. So, although I feel for die-hard typewriter users, I urge writers who are serious about marketing their work to replace their Remingtons with desktop or laptop computers.

Good printers need not be expensive but should produce quality copy. The "multipurpose" paper sold in most office supply stores is usually bright enough for professional manuscripts.

So, you need a computer, a printer, paper, and assorted other office supplies such as pens, pencils, erasers, paper clips, notepaper, post-its, and, my must-have, index cards (more about these later). You might have other "must-haves," depending upon your individual writing habits.

The Essential Bookshelf

I'm looking at the only shelf on my hutch, above the computer. On it are the main books I need to have within arm's reach at all times: a dictionary, a thesaurus, and a word usage book. Regarding the latter, find one with which you feel comfortable. This can be anything from a simple paperback such as *Merriam-Webster's Pocket Guide to English Usage* to the ponderous tome, *The Chicago Manual of Style*.

Although I still sometimes refer to my old college grammar/style book, I also purchase a new English usage book about every two years. Believe me, today's grammar "ain't your grandmother's." In other words, the "rules" change. Do you remember being taught in school that "it's either all right or all wrong" to help you remember that "all right" is two words? If you look in a dictionary or word usage book today, you'll find that "alright" is acceptable. In fact, there is a lot in writing that is acceptable today that I would have received an "F" for when I was in grade school. So do keep the most up-to-date resources.

Also on my shelf are two books specific to writing in the Christian market. One, as mentioned earlier, is Sally E. Stuart's *Christian Writers Market Guide*. The other is a book entitled *The Christian Writer's Manual of Style* (Robert Hudson, Editor)—this book will tell you how to do everything from properly cite Scripture to when to capitalize "gospel." Appendix A contains a fuller reference for both of these books.

On my other bookshelves are several different Bible versions. On last count, I had nine. Publishers often state that they want all Scripture references to be from a particular version. Today, almost every translation of the Bible can be accessed for free on the Internet. This is a boon for Christian writers (my Bible collection

Chapter 3: *In the Beginning . . .*

came about in prehistoric times, B.C.—before computers).

You might find other references helpful, too. One of my favorites is a book entitled *Where to Find It in the Bible* (Ken Anderson, Editor), an alphabetical topical concordance. I think I use this more than my regular concordance. For example, going back to the "cheating" plot in Chapter 2, if you look in this book under "cheating" you will find 14 Scripture references that address the topic of cheating—not necessarily including the word "cheating."

Now, let's move on to when and/or how often you might write.

So Much to Write, So Little Time

When I teach writing workshops, one of the questions I am asked most frequently is, "How does one find time to write?" The answer is, "You make time." When that time *is* will vary for every writer.

I'm sure you've heard that you should write every day. Must that be at the same time each day? Possibly, if it fits your schedule. Only you know when you can write. Maybe it's at 5 a.m., before the kids get up for school. Maybe it's at 11 p.m., after you get home from working second shift, or on the subway on your way to work in the morning. It may be that you can't write every day, but that you can be a "weekend writer."

I'm going to say something here with which many writers and writing instructors will disagree, but here goes: I don't think it's necessary to force yourself to sit down every day and write. There, I've said it. Everyone must develop his or her own method. We all learn differently, we all think differently, we all process differently, and we all create differently.

I am one of those writers who must have something written "in my head" before I can peck it out on the computer. So even if I am not at my computer "writing" every day at a set time, I am creating in my mind. I waste my time if I try to force something when I don't have it worked out mentally first. That's the way it is, and it works—for me.

I have other writer friends who claim not to have a "clue" on what they might write until they sit at the computer. Then, the words just seem to flow. I wish!

The point is, don't beat yourself up if you don't follow a prescribed method for setting a writing schedule. Do what works for you.

Another question I'm asked is, "Should I have a set number of hours that I write each day?" Again, only you can set such a schedule. When I first started writing, I did set a goal of writing a certain number of pages each day.

Chapter 3: *In the Beginning...*

Today, after I have a story or book plot worked out in mind, it consumes me. I sit down at the computer and can write for twelve hours straight if I'm not teaching that day. I "lose the crop," as my housemate says.

I know one writer who daily sits at his computer precisely at 6 p.m. and writes until 9 p.m. His friends and family have been forewarned against phoning, texting, or visiting him during these hours.

What will work best for you? Try a schedule you think will work. Tweak it if necessary or scrap it and begin anew. The key is to be flexible and realistic. Your writing time should be pleasant, not stressful.

<u>Prayer—Don't Begin without It</u>

I never start a writing session without praying for guidance. As Christians, we know that the Bible is the inspired word of God. I don't pretend to believe that God inspires *my* writing, but I do know He blesses my efforts.

I pray not only before I write, but also during those times I don't feel inspired. A couple years ago, I hit one of those spells where I doubted my abilities, I hadn't a writing idea in my head, and I was about to decide that the writing life was not for me. On my morning walk, I asked God directly for a story idea. I felt guilty doing this—kind of like when I prayed that the Steelers would win the Super Bowl. Surely God has better things to handle! But in my desperation, I gave my angst and "writer's block" to the Lord. By the time I got home, I had a complete story in mind. I sat at my computer and typed it in one sitting. It sold to the first magazine to which I sent it, *Bread for God's Children.*

On his website, prolific Christian children's writer Bill Myers, whose quirky books such as *My Life as a Haunted Hamburger, Hold the Pickles* entertain children of all ages, answers a reader's question about how he gets his ideas: "I try to spend 30 to 60 minutes a day with the Lord each morning, reading, praying, worshipping. It's the highlight of my day. Often the best ideas come during this time."

I hope you're getting excited about digging in and establishing your ministry to Christian children through the written word, be it writing for magazines or for the book market.

Chapter 4 begins our examination of the writing opportunities available in the Christian children's magazine market.

But first, a writing exercise for you:

Chapter 3: *In the Beginning...*

> ## Writing Exercise
> Write a prayer with which you might open your writing time.

Come, ye children, hearken unto me: I will teach you the fear of the Lord.

—Ps.34:11

Chapter 4
Christian Children's Magazines: A Treasury of Opportunity

I was raised by my grandmother, an Irish immigrant who cleaned apartment buildings to put food on our table. There was no money to buy books or magazine subscriptions.

But on my ninth birthday, my godmother gave me a subscription to a Christian children's magazine. I can't remember the name of the magazine—I'm sure it's no longer being published—but I do remember my joy when it arrived in our mailbox each month. I loved seeing it addressed to me—my very own mail! I devoured that magazine from cover to cover, and I reread it countless times until the next month's copy arrived. I felt holier after reading that magazine—I found hope and love there. Reading about God and Jesus, angels and heaven transported me from our tenement to a place I knew I wanted to be someday. I took comfort in reading about other children who struggled, too. I liked suggestions I discovered there for living a more Christ-like life. I still remember a Mother's Day issue that gave a whole list of kindnesses I could do, ways I could serve. That was the first time I'd thought that as a child of God, I should serve others—even adults!

Today's Christian children have a lot more faith-based resources on hand—DVDs and cartoons are among their favorites. But those who receive Christian magazines in the mail seem to revere them just as I did.

When birthdays come around for children and teens in my life, I almost always give them subscriptions to good Christian children's magazines that will speak to their age group and their faith journeys. These magazines are in need of good writers—why not you?

Plethora of Possibilities

Let's take a look at some of the different types of writing that Christian children's magazine editors might seek from freelance writers. In subsequent chapters, we will go into depth on writing in many of these areas. This list is by no means exhaustive, but represents most of what you'll find in Christian children's magazines:

Chapter 4: *Christian Children's Magazines*

- Short stories
- Feature articles
- Devotions
- Personal experience articles
- Faith testimonies
- Crafts
- Recipes
- Puzzles
- Games
- Activities
- Plays/Skits/Puppet plays
- Bible stories
- Rebuses
- Biographies
- Profiles
- Poetry
- Humor
- Quizzes

Obviously, not every Christian children's magazine will contain all these features. Much depends upon the mission of the magazine and the age of readership. For example, if a magazine is a denominational supplement for a preschool Sunday school curriculum, it may contain one fiction story, followed by a few questions that help readers apply the lesson learned; a Scripture reading that is the basis of that week's lesson; and perhaps a coloring page that correlates to the Scripture passage. Even small publications such as this need to be written by somebody! Again, why not by you?

Be Informed—What You Need to Know before Submitting Work to a Magazine

In Chapter 2, we talked in general terms about the need to know the markets. Never is this more important than when writing for magazines.

When writing a book, you have control over its voice and style; when writing for a magazine, you need to match your writing to its "tone."

Of course, your two starting points in getting to know a particular magazine you would like to target are to read its guidelines and read at least one sample copy (preferably more).

In addition to the basic questions of "what can I submit?" (such as fiction, nonfiction, etc.), the key questions this research should answer for you include:

- Which age group does this magazine target?

- Does it target both genders?

Chapter 4: *Christian Children's Magazines*

- Is it a denominational or nondenominational publication?

    If it's a denominational magazine, do I have sufficient knowledge of the beliefs of this denomination to make a credible contribution?

    For example, let's say you've plotted a story in which a young girl has been charged with keeping her dress clean until it's time to go to church for her baby brother's baptism. Not all Christian denominations baptize infants.

    Know the beliefs of a denomination before attempting to write for one of its publications.

- Is this a themed magazine and, if so, how can I get a copy of the theme list and deadlines for submission?

    Writing for themed magazines gives writers a "leg up"—you are not shooting in the dark when it comes to developing a story and deciding on its theme. You already know that your story will revolve around a predetermined theme such as "families" or "peer pressure."

- If I'm writing fiction, how much "religion" should I include? Do I have to mention God if the good moral message comes through anyway? Reading your targeted magazine's fiction should answer that question for you.

- If I include Scripture, must it come from a particular Bible translation?

    Often you can get this information in the magazine's "masthead." This is usually a boxed area that contains information on the owner of the publication, its editorial staff, possibly circulation information, and other information that children won't read but that can offer an abundance of help to prospective writers.

    For example, *SHINE brightly*, a magazine for Christian girls 9-to-14-years-old, has a very informative masthead, including the statement that all quoted Scripture contained in its stories and articles are taken from the New International Version of the Bible.

- What is the magazine's mission?

    Many times this is stated in the writer's guidelines. It might be stated in the masthead, too.

    Again using *SHINE brightly* as an example, they clearly state their mission on their masthead, which includes the facts that their readership is female, and that their mission is to help girls under-

Chapter 4: *Christian Children's Magazines*

stand how God is working in their lives as well as in the world around them.

- And, of course, there is one more question that deserves its own section...

<u>Will I Get Paid?</u>

A graduate from a writing course I teach recently emailed me with a dilemma. She had sent a manuscript to a Christian magazine and it was accepted. The problem? "They don't pay except in contributor copies," she wrote. "Should I hold out and try to sell it to a publisher that pays? I know I want to minister through my writing, but I need to make some money too, even if it's just a little." Even though I had to give her one of those "ultimately it's your decision" type answers, I did try to encourage her to not feel guilty for wanting payment for her labors—there certainly is precedent for this in the Bible.

Most magazine publishers are financed by subscriptions and advertising. This is also true to some extent in the Christian magazine market. However, many, especially children's magazines, do not include advertising. Rather, they depend on subscriptions, donations, and/or funding from ministries that are part of a larger non-profit organization. For example, *Bread for God's Children*, a family publication that contains stories for children, includes in its masthead the facts that it is interdenominational, is supported by Bread Ministries, Inc., and is not subsidized by any particular church, individual, group or organization. Other Christian magazines state this type information in their mastheads.

For the most part, Christian children's magazines do pay at a lower rate than do secular children's magazines. Some pay in copies only. Others may just state "no payment." However, if we writers have done our homework and studied the writers' guidelines, we should know in advance the publisher's terms.

If you want to get paid, then do not submit your work to a market that you know does not pay.

I do need to earn money from my writing; however, if I write a story that I know would be perfect for a nonpaying Christian children's magazine, I do not hesitate to send it to the publisher. I consider it the "giving" part of my ministry.

Chapter 4: *Christian Children's Magazines*

Do I Have to Write for Magazines before Writing for the Book Market?

This is another of those "FAQs"—frequently-asked questions. The answer is "no"; the beauty of being a freelance writer is that you have the freedom to write what you wish and send it to the market of your choice.

But before you begin the year-long or longer commitment of writing a young adult novel, consider this: publishers are more likely to review manuscripts submitted by writers with publishing credits. If you can get a publishing credit or two in the Christian children's magazine market, go for it. You can keep manuscripts circulating while you're working on that book.

In the next chapter, we'll delve into the different types of Christian children's fiction that magazine editors will consider. Do you have a project in mind?

Before you answer that question, here's an exercise for you:

Writing Exercise

Identify a Christian children's magazine known to you now or remembered from childhood. What features from that magazine did you most enjoy as a child or do you think a child would most enjoy (examples include stories, articles,

Sowing Seeds

> Bible quizzes, crafts, plays, etc.). Why did you choose that feature? Would you enjoy writing such a feature?

...Jesus said, "Suffer little children, and forbid them not to come unto me, for of such is the kingdom of heaven."

—Matt. 19:14

Chapter 5
The Joy of Short Fiction

I still have notes from my senior seminar in fiction writing that I took at the University of Pittsburgh many moons ago. The definition of "fiction" I scribbled down is, "Fiction is literature that is the product of its writer's imagination, usually not based in fact." While this simple definition is certainly the core of fiction, it doesn't satisfy all that writers want to know before venturing into the world of creating this literary form. It seems that the "usually not based in fact" is the major sticking point. Some FAQs my students ask include:

- Can I use the real name of a town or city for my setting?

- Can I base my characters on real people if I give them different names?

- What if I add dialogue when I'm retelling a Bible story. Does that make the whole story fiction?

- I've heard that fiction is based on our own experiences. Is this true?

- Can I use a talking animal as my main character in preschool or young reader stories for Christian magazines?

The answer to all these questions is "possibly"... You can use a real town or city for your setting as long as the setting details you include are accurate...Most of our characters are based in part on people we know or have observed, but our writer's imagination will have to create what we don't know about those persons (such as what they think) in order to develop three dimensional, memorable characters...Generally adding anything to a Bible story makes it fiction... Story plots can be seeded with a personal experience but, again, our writer's imagination needs to invent a plot around it... Most Christian children's magazines feature fiction with "real" children as opposed to talking animals, although I've never seen a "rule" about this. I think perhaps this is because as Christians, we believe that we are the only ones of God's creation with souls. However, I have seen talking animal stories in excellent preschool

Chapter 5: *The Joy of Short Fiction*

Christian children's magazines such as Focus on the Family's *Clubhouse Jr*. These are stories with a good moral message but that don't have the animals attending Sunday school or reading the Bible.

The most common type of fiction you will write for magazines is short stories. We will spend most of our discussion on this genre.

<u>Writing Christian Children's Short Stories</u>

Recently I was one of several speakers at a high school career day. During the question and answer period, one girl asked me, "Do you ever want to be a professional writer—you know, like for adults?" This is the type reaction we children's writers often encounter. I tried to explain the challenge of writing meaningful stories in so few words; but I could see the unbelief in my questioner's face—and I thought back to my own school days, when the 500 word essay seemed like a torturous assignment. Surely 100 words would be easier! Not. Writing short fiction for children is not for the faint of heart.

Elements of Short Stories

There are entire books available on how to write short fiction. Here, I'll summarize what I think are the important aspects you need to consider. Short stories for Christian children need to contain basic fiction elements of:

Plot

What happens in your story? (For example, George wants to go fishing but he's promised to help clean his grandfather's house. He fights with his conscience and finally discovers a way to meet his obligations and also have fun.)

Be sure your plot has a faith element. Etta G. Martin, editor of *Partners*, advises, "Each of our stories needs to teach a spiritual lesson, and it is often portrayed through the dialogue and actions of the story's characters. Parents and teachers (in the story) may use Scripture to help children understand an issue, but large amounts of Scripture should not be quoted." She and other editors of Christian children's magazines advocate avoiding "preaching" by adult characters and allowing the young protagonists to think for themselves.

A final word on plot: be original. According to Martin, the biggest reason fiction manuscripts are rejected by *Partners* is that "they tell a story we've heard and heard before, and the scanty clothes used to cover the same old skeleton neither camouflage it nor make it attractive to readers because its outcome is too predictable."

Theme

What universal truth do you want your story to convey? What is the "take away" message for readers? For example, perhaps you have written a story based on the theme, "As Christians we are called to serve."

Characters

Most children's short stories contain one protagonist—usually your point-of-view character (should be a child, the same age as or a year or two older than your audience), perhaps one more character with a major role (such as a close friend or a sibling), and one or two minor characters.

When writing short fiction, you don't have the luxury of developing a huge cast of characters.

Remember: In children's fiction, for the most part, adults should have very minor roles.

Conflict

What must your protagonist overcome? This can be anything from nature (such as surviving a tornado) to another human being (for example, dealing with a bully or with an overbearing older sibling) to the child him or herself (for example, wondering where God is during a tumultuous time at home).

Note that your protagonist should also be the one to resolve the conflict, although they can have some adult assistance.

Setting—Time and Place

It's important for readers to know where your story takes place in time; it can be contemporary, historical, or futuristic.

Regardless, though, your timeline should be short—you don't have room to adequately develop a story that spans years. In a short story, it's more like one day or a week or two.

The place setting is important only as it impacts the story. For example, if you are writing a contemporary story about a child not wanting to clean her room, readers don't need to know on what street or in which city she lives.

However, if you're writing a biblical fiction story about a shepherd boy watching Jesus

Chapter 5: *The Joy of Short Fiction*

carrying the cross, then names of places are pertinent, as in any historical fiction.

The Structure of a Short Story

Your story structure is important and consists of:

Beginning

The beginning should be short, introduce your main character(s), and begin with action and at the point where your story conflict is about to be disclosed. Here is the opening to one of my stories, "The Truth of the Matter" (*Bread for God's Children*, Issue 2, 2006):

> Jessie Sanchez barely scribbled the English homework assignment in his notebook before the dismissal bell rang. He grabbed his backpack and sprinted down the hall.
> "Man!" he gasped, catching up with his best friend, Seth. "I thought that class would never end. And homework! Who said sixth grade would be a snap?"
> Seth grinned. "That's what you get for being in the gifted program."

Sowing Seeds

> The boys hurried to the gym to change for basketball practice. As Jessie laced his high-tops, his mind raced down the list of things he had to do—a book report for English, his science fair project, a report on Ponce de Leon for Social Studies, and a poster for his church youth rally. Some of these projects had been assigned before Christmas, and Jessie had intended to do them over winter break. But a guy had to relax! He'd spent his vacation playing basketball and watching football.

In an opening such as this, we meet the main characters, learn something about the protagonist (he's about 12 years old, likeable, smart, athletic, a procrastinator, and a Christian), and we have an idea about the conflict to come—conflict to which many readers will relate, the consequences of not setting priorities. Shortly, readers will see added to that conflict the decision Jessie must make between honesty and dishonesty to get himself out of the trouble caused by his procrastination.

Middle

The middle advances the plot, presents obstacles for your protagonist to overcome (there are

Chapter 5: *The Joy of Short Fiction*

some fiction books that give a "formula"—say, three attempts and three failures before success, but this is not something to which I always adhere), and builds to a climax—that moment of conflict resolution.

In "The Truth of the Matter," Jessie's athletic prowess and classroom performance both take a tumble. His parents will not let him drop the gifted program, which he thinks is the root of his problem. In his desperation to finish his homework, Jessie finds an old encyclopedia from which he copies some paragraphs for his Ponce De Leon report. He gets caught, he's grounded from everything but youth group, and he's angry.

Then as he's hanging banners for the youth rally, he finds one about truth that reads, "If you can't be true to yourself, you can't be true to God." This leads to Jessie's "aha" moment, the climax. (Some books will put the climax as part of the ending—I think of it as the ending of the middle.)

Ending

The ending should be short and share with readers the outcome, the result of having resolved the conflict. How has it changed your protagonist? This needn't be a "total makeover"—often it's a new awareness, or a boost in self-confidence.

In my story, Jessie seeks out his youth group leader (to whom he's already told his story) and asks if he should see if his teacher will let him redo the report. After Jim encourages this, the last line in the story is:

> Jessie grinned. "I'll see her tomorrow. Being grounded for two weeks, I'll have time to write the world's best report!"

We see that Jessie's good humor has returned, that he has taken responsibility for his actions, and that we assume he will learn to balance (prioritize) his responsibilities with his fun times.

Story Structure and Age Groups

Before we leave the world of short stories, let's look at their structure in terms of the age groups you will target.

Chapter 5: *The Joy of Short Fiction*

Preschoolers

Keep plots and themes simple. Write clearly and succinctly. Include plenty of action. Chronological timelines (no flashbacks) usually work best for these little ones. Keep word length short. Faith concepts should be basic—we go to church, we pray at home and at church, Jesus loves us and we love Jesus.

Primary Grades/Beginner Readers

Plots and themes can be a little more complex and reflect these kids' expanding world. Straightforward writing is still best, with the plot unfolding in a chronological manner. Children in this age group are more aware of right and wrong; they are developing their own "moral compass." Violence should not be part of their stories. Mysteries should revolve around fairly benign "cases"—a lost cat, a missing jewelry box, an empty house in which a lamp comes on each night.

Middle Graders

Action and adventure are key for these readers. Many adult publications are written at a fifth grade reading level, so you needn't be as aware of vocabulary level and sentence structure as you will be when writing for younger readers. Christian middle grade readers enjoy all genres. They are developing a social awareness, and certainly your plots can reflect this. Fantasy is particularly enjoyed by middle graders—but, be aware, some Christian denominations discourage fantasy; some consider Halloween a pagan holiday and others feel that since a birth date for Jesus is not stated in Scripture, Christmas is not a true Christian celebration; some will not accept ghost stories. Know your markets!

Teens/Young Adults

It is getting more difficult to find good Christian teen magazines; many have ceased publication. Teens (also called young adults) usually want fiction that reflects their real worlds, plots in which the protagonist must stand up against drugs, sexual promiscuity, and other modern day social situations in which their faith is tested. They want emotion in their stories. One trend in this market is for publishers to seek fiction written by teens, so before submitting your story to a Christian teen publication, read a copy. Often there are a photo, name, and age of the author, if a teen. Note that vocabulary is about that of the adult market for this age group; however, keeping dialogue "real" is particularly

Chapter 5: *The Joy of Short Fiction*

needed for this age group. Might today's teen greet another with, "How do you do, sir?" or "Yo, dude!"

Other Short Fiction Opportunities

Following is a sampling of other short fiction opportunities:

Retold Bible Stories

These are considered fiction because usually dialogue and other information are added in order to make a Scripture selection more "kid-friendly."

Suppositions are made—for example, if I were retelling the story of Mary's visit to Elizabeth, I might write something like, "Mary probably grew weary, making such a long trip on foot."

The degree of fictionalization allowed in Bible stories varies widely among Christian children's magazines. Some may only allow the addition of dialogue and "suppositions" based on fact—the way we know it was in Bible times. Otherwise, no "new" characters can be added.

Other magazines allow more liberal changes, such as the addition of characters not in the original Scripture—for example, perhaps a writer might create a companion for Mary on her journey to visit her cousin, so that dialogue created between Mary and that companion will make Mary a more three-dimensional character.

In all cases, the message in the chosen Scripture passages must remain true and must "play out" in your story.

Plays/Skits/Puppet Shows

Some Christian children's magazines seek short "drama" that can be performed in Sunday school or in a group setting.

Playwright Yvonne Robert suggests first conceiving your play as you would a short story, with all the elements of good fiction. Then you can format it as a play, to include: separating your story into scenes and acts, correctly parenthesizing your characters' actions, correctly setting up and punctuating the dialogue. Since the narrative of a play is spoken, no quotation marks are needed.

Here is a sample of how your play might begin:

(The angel stands at the foot of Ricky's bed. She gently grabs his toe. Ricky rubs his eyes and sits up in bed.)

Chapter 5: *The Joy of Short Fiction*

>Angel: Good morning, Ricky. Do you remember me from your dream?
>Ricky (frowning): I think so—were you the good angel or the bad angel?

This format is the same for plays, skits, or puppet shows. Skits are usually just one scene or one act. These are more likely to be used in a Sunday school class. Writing scripts is an art in itself. Be sure to study some before attempting one, yourself.

Rebus

Rebuses are sometimes also called "picture stories." These are generally for preschool readers. Pictures can be substituted for some words or be positioned before or after them. Nouns work best as the pictures, with usually the only non-nouns used being, perhaps, colors or numbers. Rebuses are short, seldom more than 125 words—yet they need to be complete stories. Here is how a rebus line might look:

>The sun (picture of sun) rose above the tree (picture of tree) by John's church (picture of church).

Or,

The (picture of sun) rose above the (picture of tree) by John's (picture of church).

Rebuses may be the trickiest 125 words you'll ever write! Those in Christian children's magazines should, of course, contain a faith element.

You'll be happy to know that the magazine's art department will supply the rebus pictures, but you need to indicate what the rebus pictures should be. You can do this on the top of the rebus when you submit it.

Summary

So, there you have it. If you love to write fiction and you love the Lord, writing fiction for Christian children's magazines might be the ministry for you. Give it a try!

Our next chapter is an overview of nonfiction in Christian children's magazines. I've heard it said that it is "easier" to sell nonfiction; I don't believe this to be true, although I will agree that there are more opportunities in nonfiction.

Before you move on, try your hand at the following exercise:

Chapter 5: *The Joy of Short Fiction*

> ## *Writing Exercise*
> Create a plot summary for the age group of your choice. What will be the theme of your story? What faith element will your plot include, if any? (for example, will your protagonist go to church during one of the scenes, read the Bible, mention a service project for her youth group?) If no explicit faith element is planned, what Christian value would your plot portray?

While ye have light, believe in the light, that ye may be the children of light.

—John 12:36

Chapter 6

The Challenge—and Blessing—of Nonfiction

"Why do I have to write a nonfiction article?" whined one of my students. "I never plan to write nonfiction. It's boring!" His sentiment has been repeated over the years by many of my adult writing students, who often view the one nonfiction piece (out of a total of ten assignments) that they must produce as a necessary evil toward earning the course credits. Many fear the research that may be involved. Others just repeat the "B" word—boring!

Axing the Yawn Factor

I attended Catholic schools, way back when nuns taught. I stood in awe of these women who dwelled behind convent walls and whose lives consisted of work and prayer. Whenever I hear the word "bored," I think back to Sister Anne Therese, my eighth grade teacher. One day after school while helping her put up a bulletin board, I asked, "Sister, don't you get bored being a nun, never getting out or having fun?" Her laughter tinkled like wind chimes. "My dear, even after all my years in the convent, each morning when the bell rings for prayer, I praise God for the privilege of waking to another day to serve Him. I love every minute of my life. That's what I want for all my students, Kathleen. If you make your life work something about which you are passionate, I promise that you'll never be bored."

Sister was right, and I experience the wisdom of her words not just in my life but in everything I write. Never is this more true than when writing nonfiction for children, which must be every bit as interesting as fiction.

Be passionate about your topic. If you don't give a hoot about honey bees and why their numbers have decreased, please don't write about it. Choose a topic about which you already care or one about which you are itching to learn more.

When writing articles for Christian children, your own love for Christ must shine through every word you pen.

Nonfiction in Christian children's magazines covers everything that "is not fiction," including articles, games, puzzles, devotions, and so forth. Basically, nonfiction articles are

Chapter 6: Nonfiction

"factual," not a product of the writer's imagination, but rather information that writers present in an interesting, unique, informative matter. Nonfiction writers must be able to substantiate the facts they include either from sources or from their own expertise.

Obviously, as your magazine analyses will show, there are many more opportunities for submitting nonfiction than fiction. We will go into depth on articles and then briefly discuss the many other nonfiction opportunities in the Christian children's magazine market.

<u>Writing Nonfiction Children's Articles from a Christian Perspective</u>

We've already determined that your article topic will be something about which you are passionate. But what do Christian children's magazines include in their nonfiction? Must everything be about God or Jesus?

As with Christian children's fiction, their nonfiction does not necessarily have to be "religious" or "theological" in nature, but it must directly or indirectly point readers to the glory of God.

And as always, your choice of topic depends on the market you target. For example, there is a terrific Christian children's magazine,

Nature Friend, which publishes a variety of nature-related articles that may or may not mention God or include Scripture. Yet all the articles are written with the "awe" factor that leads readers to explore the wonders within God's creation, which is the stated mission of this publication.

What else can you write about? One popular topic is "life choice" type articles. These are usually interactive, involving readers. Perhaps you present two scenarios—say a child finding a lost dog; in one scenario, the child hides the dog in his room and keeps it; in the other, the child and parents put up posters and try to find the owner. Which would readers do? Your article could then go on to give Scripture support for making an honest choice.

Another often-sought article is a profile. You might write such an article based on your interview with a young Christian; perhaps a child in your church has overcome physical challenges, or another has developed a unique ministry—there are oodles of "good" kids out there whose stories would inspire other young Christians.

You can write a biography on someone, past or present, whose story inspires you. It is important when writing such biographies to include childhood and young adult information of your subject's life, which will be of particular

Chapter 6: Nonfiction

interest to young readers. And of course, your subject must be a good Christian role model.

Truly, the subject matter for Christian children's articles is vast. And at the risk of sounding like a stuck CD, magazine guidelines should indeed be your guide. For example, Editor Etta G. Martin (*Partners*) specifies their need for nonfiction articles this way: "We use articles on these themes: nature, Biblical and/or Anabaptist history, customs or information about other times and cultures as they relate to Biblical truth or aid in understanding of Bible accounts. No theological credentials are required to supply nonfiction articles, but the articles should point out a spiritual lesson the reader can learn from the subject." Now, that's specific!

Depending on the age of your audience, you can write about missions and missionaries, social issues, careers, hints for school success, or personal experiences (I still remember an article in a Christian children's magazine about a family that lived on a houseboat for a year and the effect it had on their family life and faith journeys).

As stated above, editorial guidelines will give you general or specific subject categories which will generate lots of ideas. Just remember this when choosing your topic: from the time your article is accepted for publication to the time it appears in that publication, a year or more will probably elapse. This will affect the wording of your article; instead of stating, for example, "Children flocked to the Angel Cadets concert last week..." you would write "Children flocked to an Angel Cadets concert in June, 2010."

Also remember that when an issue is "hot," editors are bombarded with articles (and fiction) revolving around that topic. For example, at the time of this writing, we are hearing in the media a lot about bullying. My students' stories and articles are replete with this theme and so, according to editors, are the manuscripts submitted to publishers. I actually saw in a publisher's online guidelines this statement: "Please! No articles on bullying—we are overstocked."

When you are zeroing in on a topic for a Christian children's article, ask yourself these questions:

- Am I passionate about this topic?

- Will children care about this topic and, if so, for which age group will I target my article?

- How will my article differ from those already published on this topic?

- Is there a market for an article such as this?

Chapter 6: *Nonfiction*

- If my topic is "popular" right now, how will I slant my article to make it unique and fresh?

Anatomy of an Article

If you wish to "reel in" readers, you must start your article with a bang. Let's say that I am writing a biography on a young boy who unwittingly became a hero during the 1991 coup d'etat in Haiti (for the purposes of this example, I'm creating the boy, although the event is factual). I would probably start like this:

> For Louis Dupree, September 30, 1991 began like any other day in his Haitian village. He'd awakened early, helped Mammi pack the cart to haul vegetables to the market, and started weeding the sweet potato patch. Suddenly, an explosion sounded in the valley below. Louis watched in horror as thin streams of smoke wafted up the mountain. They seemed to be coming from the Presidential Palace…

Now, this biography could have begun, "Louis Dupree was born in 1980 in Jacmel, Haiti…" Yawn. I can promise you that young

Sowing Seeds

readers will move on to something else. Be creative with your openings.

Another way to start an article is with a believable scenario. Suppose you are writing a factual teen article on a newly discovered danger of smoking marijuana. You might want to open with a scenario like this, which directly addresses readers:

> You're leaving a party at 11:45 p.m. and need to hustle to get home by your midnight curfew. You feel surprisingly alert, given the couple puffs you took of somebody's joint. "You're cool to drive," your friend assures you. "Weed doesn't affect you like alcohol."
>
> You're almost home when approaching headlights blind you. They seem brighter than sunlight. You jerk the steering wheel to the right and a tree seems to leap out at you. "Dear God," you cry. Then the airbag explodes in your face.
>
> Your friend was wrong. Recent tests conducted by the Coalition to Study Effects of Marijuana show that marijuana heightens sensory perception to the point that...

In the example above, your first two paragraphs are meant to "hook" readers; the third para-

Chapter 6: Nonfiction

graph introduces your topic more specifically. (Please note that for the purpose of this example, I invented the Coalition and its study.)

Once you have captured the interest of your readers, the middle of your article had better live up to the "hype" of the beginning. This is the "meat" of the topic, where you present everything about your topic you want readers to know. Nonetheless, this part of your article should not be encyclopedic; include anecdotes wherever possible. Involve readers by directly addressing them. Organize your article such that it flows well and is easily understood; use subheadings as an article "map," if appropriate.

Above all, keep your article focused. For example, if I were writing the teen article above, I would not include the history of marijuana, where it's grown, etc.—I would keep the information I include focused on the effects marijuana might have on users' five senses.

The best way to get the "feel" of how to write Christian children's nonfiction is to read several magazine articles, particularly those in children's magazines for which you might write.

Article endings are generally a summary of the information presented in the article and often contain a "takeaway" message. For example, the teen article conceived above might end like this:

The adverse effect marijuana can have on our senses is frightening—and can be life-altering. The message that smoking weed is "harmless" is just plain wrong, even though friends may try to convince us otherwise. Even Jesus was tempted during his lifetime (Luke 4:2-13), and we will be, too. Pray for the strength to resist such temptations. Don't wait until your car is headed for a tree to cry out, "Dear God!"

A Word about Research

"Research" is not a dirty word—in fact, you might come to enjoy this phase of writing nonfiction. I love research!

Whether or not it is necessary depends upon what you are writing. If you're writing a profile, the information you obtain by interviewing your subject will be sufficient, unless you want to include other pertinent facts. Let's say you have written a profile on a boy who participates in Special Olympics and you want to include a tidbit, say, on the different categories of competition. That would be an item to research, probably on the official Special Olympics website.

Chapter 6: *Nonfiction*

Personal experience articles do not require research.

But almost every other type of article will require that you consult reliable sources from which you will extract information to include in your article. Your library is the best place to start. For research in Christian books such as Bible commentaries, you can go to your church library or your pastor's office or a local Christian college or seminary.

I also like to consult cumulative magazine indexes, where possible, as well as the *Readers' Guide to Periodical Literature* before I start a nonfiction project to see what has already been written on my topic and to help me plan my article so it will give a different slant or update on the subject.

The Internet has changed the way we writers conduct research. However, we must use this wonder of technology with due diligence. Sites such as Wikipedia—to which anyone can post information—are not considered accurate by publishers. Look for websites with .edu, .org, and/or .gov URL suffixes—these are usually factual.

When writing a biography, try to access "primary sources" such as diaries or letters written by your subject.

Interviews with experts are excellent sources for nonfiction articles. For example, if you are writing an article on the okapi, one of

God's particularly unique creatures, you might interview a zookeeper who is in charge of an okapi breeding program. For Bible experts, your pastor might be able to help or suggest theologians for you to contact.

There are books written on proper ways to research and how to prepare a bibliography to catalogue the sources you've used. Note that nonfiction articles for children are not academic research papers; you will not have footnotes, and your bibliography will not appear at the end of the article—you include it for the editor, whose "fact checkers" will use it to verify the information you included in your article. When I write nonfiction, I try to find at least two sources for each fact I include.

Some Legal Considerations...

Publishers—and even legal experts—vary on how much writers can or cannot quote from published material before they need to get permission from the author or publishers, even when properly cited. Some sources give an arbitrary number, say up to 50 words, that a writer can quote in his or her work without obtaining permission. To err on the side of safety, I endeavor to get permission to include any direct quote or excerpt, unless it comes

Chapter 6: *Nonfiction*

from "a public domain" source, such as the Robert Frost poem quoted in this book. There are legal guides for writers that discuss this and other such aspects of publishing; one is referenced in Appendix A. These can serve as a guide, but ultimately let your editor tell you the policy of his or her publication and determine whether it is the responsibility of the writer or the publisher to obtain any needed permissions. Just be sure as you write your article that you keep careful notes for bibliographical information.

Also—and this is not arbitrary, whenever you interview and/or photograph a minor you must have parental/guardian permission (in writing). I also make it mandatory for an adult to be present when I'm interviewing a child.

Non-article Nonfiction

Now, let's briefly discuss some of the other nonfiction you might consider—I guarantee, you'll enjoy trying any or all of these types of writing.

Crafts/Recipes

Children love making things, and crafts and recipes are included in many preschool, primary and middle-grade reader Christian magazines (not so much for teens).

Craft and recipe how-to's are generally set up the same: a brief introduction (one sentence), a list of materials or ingredients, a numbered list of instructions for making the item, and a brief closure (one sentence). Seldom do craft or recipe articles fill more than half a page in a magazine.

Keep in mind that the materials or ingredients needed should be readily available in most homes and classrooms; such items as porcelain beads that have to be purchased at a craft store or an exotic spice should not be on the list.

The instructions must be age appropriate—a craft for preschoolers, for example, should not include a step that calls for cutting with a razor blade.

Christian children's magazines particularly like crafts that can be correlated with a Sunday school lesson or Scripture passage. Be sure your idea is original, not something you've found in a craft pattern book. Likewise, recipes might correlate with a story or article in the magazine, or with a season—a December issue

Chapter 6: Nonfiction

of a Christian preschool magazine might contain a recipe for making marshmallow angels.

Poetry

Many Christian children's magazines need good, short poetry. In the interest of interaction, many such magazines only publish poetry written by their young readers. But there is a market for submissions from adult contributors. Being poetry-challenged myself, I stand in awe of those who can express their love of Jesus through their poetry. If you're one of those writers that God has gifted with a poetic bent, this may be just the genre for your ministry. Be sure to read several Christian children's magazines that accept poetry so you can begin to get a "feel" for what is published.

Quizzes/Word Games/Puzzles

Secular and Christian children's magazines usually devote a lot of space to activities such as word games, puzzles, and quizzes. I have written quizzes, and I love doing word games and puzzles, but I am not good at creating and constructing them.

So Christian author and puzzle creator Evelyn Christensen has been gracious enough to share with you her expertise in this area. As to which type puzzle/word game appeals most to which age group, Christensen says that children "...have diverse abilities and diverse interests, so they're not all going to like the same kind of puzzles. Some...are very visually oriented and like visual puzzles best, some are strong in math and like number and logic puzzles best, and some are good with words and like those kinds of puzzles."

Of course, editors of magazines for Christian children publish the type of puzzles, games, and quizzes that have historically appealed most to their readership.

Preschool puzzles are often visual, such as one that presents four drawings of baby Jesus in the manger and asks readers to match two that are identical. Christensen adds that mazes also appeal to these little ones.

Primary and middle graders are open to anything, from Bible word searches and crosswords to mazes to Bible fill-ins. Intermediate readers also enjoy codes and logic grids, according to Christensen.

Teen Christian magazines may contain an occasional crossword, sudoku, or acrostic, but quizzes, often life choice in nature, are more often used by some publishers. For example, a fall 2008 issue of *Ignite Your Faith* (formerly *Campus Life*) includes a quiz, "Are You Living Your Faith?" by Amy Adair. Readers are pre-

Chapter 6: Nonfiction

sented with 15 scenarios that teens will encounter in their daily lives, such as whether or not to forgive perceived wrongs by ex-friends. Readers are given three possible actions for each of the scenarios, from which they are instructed to select one. There is a scoring guide based on readers' answers to show them where they are when it comes to living their Christian faith.

Should puzzles, quizzes, and word games be "easy"? Veteran puzzle writer Evelyn Christensen says not: "I think readers prefer a puzzle to be challenging, but just as teachers need to plan their lessons so they're hard enough to stretch their students' thinking, but not so hard that their students get discouraged and give up, so puzzle designers must find that delicate balance. Readers seldom like a puzzle that's really easy."

When asked which type of puzzle is most difficult to design, Christensen states, "For me, the toughest kind to create well is the hidden picture puzzle, the kind where you have a complex picture with all kinds of small pictures cleverly concealed with the larger picture. I have great respect for the people who create those, and those puzzles happen to be one of my favorite kinds to solve."

Mine, too!

If you wish to try your hand at this type of writing/designing, study the magazine you plan to target and see which quizzes, word games and/or puzzles it includes. When you submit your manuscript, be sure to include a completed puzzle as an answer key for the editor. Have fun!

Devotions

I love writing devotions, and throughout my freelance career have written them for devotional magazines for both children and adults.

Some Christian children's magazines use devotions in conjunction with other genres (such as stories and articles) and others may be entirely devoted to devotions that can be read daily. Each such devotional magazine covers a period of time, say two to three months.

Devotions usually expand on Scripture passages. A typical format is to first present the Scripture passage, followed by the writer's discussion on that passage, followed by a brief prayer or application for it.

Devotions and Scripture applications for children must be age appropriate and meaningful for their stage in life and in their faith journeys.

Activities

If you are a parent or teacher, you know how important it is to keep children occupied.

Activities in Christian children's magazines can be anything from a game (apart from "paper and pencil" games—perhaps a unique treasure hunt) to ideas for a fundraising project. As with crafts and recipes, these should use readily-available items if materials are required.

Older children's magazines often welcome service ideas, such as packing shoeboxes with school supplies and prayer cards or tracts and then sending them to a mission.

Can sleepovers be planned to have a Christian theme? I'll bet there is a creative writer out there right now who is writing an article detailing just such an activity.

You can even write an article on a possible "field trip" activity for a youth group, such as one detailing ways to share faith with those in nursing homes.

Columns/Departments

If you're a regular reader of a particular magazine, you'll note that there are certain features that are always written by the same person. Freelance writers will not submit material to these columns or departments.

BUT, you can submit an idea for a new column. In fact, I did just that after reading a magazine, *Action*, put out by United Spinal Association. It is written for persons of all ages who have physical disabilities, as I do. I saw a need, though, for something just for children. So, I wrote up a couple of sample columns targeted at children with disabilities. I sent them off with a proposal for a column I titled "Kids in Action." At this writing, I am about to begin my fifth year as columnist for this magazine. So, we can create our own opportunities.

Let's say you're reading a children's magazine put out by your Christian denomination. You like it, but you see the need for more "practical" Scripture applications for its 9-to-12-year-old readers. Perhaps you envision a feature (written by you, of course) in each issue titled "Lessons Learned" which will give, say, five everyday life applications of a particular Scripture passage. Write up a sample column and draft a cover letter. Give the editor your rationale for wanting to include this new feature in the magazine. Express your enthusiasm and availability for writing it. Who knows, you might soon be a columnist!

Fillers

I just want to add a word here about "fillers." These are very short pieces that publishers use to fill spaces on magazine pages. Not too many children's magazines use these. However, as you'll see in Sally E. Stuart's *Christian Writer's*

Chapter 6: *Nonfiction*

Market Guide, there are markets for fillers. These can be anything from true, funny anecdotes to trivia to a nifty quotation that has spoken to your heart. The small checks you can accumulate by writing for this market can really add up!

A Word about Drafts

Before we leave our discussion on writing nonfiction, I want to conclude with a word about "drafts." As you revise an article, you might decide to cut something you've included that, on second reading, seems a bit out of focus. Go ahead and cut it, but don't throw away that bit of writing or any research you've saved related to it. My friend and writing colleague Judy Woller advises, "I keep a "Bits & Pieces" file for each project and place anything in it that I cut. Maybe I can use it later or in another piece of writing."

Summary

I hope by now you are excited over the possibility of writing nonfiction for Christian children's magazines. It is immensely satisfying to know that something you've written will inform a child or teen as they grow in their love of Jesus Christ. Bear in mind that once an editor accepts your manuscript, it is probable that he or she will want to see more of your work. The more you write and the more you submit your work, the stronger your ministry will grow.

In the next chapter, we'll begin to explore the other major publishing outlet for Christian children's writers: books.

But first, try your hand at the following exercise:

Writing Exercise

Write a paragraph or two summarizing an article you might explore writing for a Christian children's magazine. Include the age group it would target, and your rationale for thinking your article topic will interest your readership. Do you have a magazine market in mind?

Even a child is known by his doings,
whether his work be pure,
and whether it be right.

—Prov.20:11

Chapter 7
Christian Children's Books— Storehouses of Faith Seeds

"A good book is the precious life-blood of a master spirit, embalmed and treasured up on purpose to a life beyond life," author John Milton said in his oft-quoted speech against censorship, delivered in England in 1644. When we write Christian children's books, we aim for that high standard—that our words will indeed be treasured by and sowers of faith seeds in our readers.

Have you made that visit yet to a Christian bookstore? If not, try to go today. I want you to be inspired by what has already been published, get excited about adopting writing in this genre as your ministry, and perhaps get ideas for what has yet to be written—by you.

Crystal Bowman, author of over two dozen beginning readers and over forty picture books in the Christian children's market, says of her ministry, "What I try to teach through my books for young children is that God is part of their everyday lives and he loves and cares for them very much. Some of my books have a stronger evangelical message which includes the story of Jesus' death and resurrection. It all depends on the genre and purpose of each title, but they all include some spiritual message even if it is subtle."

Prepare to Immerse Yourself

I recently had the most interesting conversation with an aspiring young writer. I was one of the "critiquers" (I just made up this word—writers do that sometimes!) at a "nuts and bolts of writing for children" workshop. Attendees had submitted up to ten-page manuscripts to be critiqued by published authors, and I had received this fellow's short story. I tried to tell him—diplomatically, of course—that while he had some good ideas, his plot did not flow well nor did it lead to a satisfactory conclusion.

"I know," he said. "I just threw this together so I could meet with you to talk about my book idea—well, books, really. I have this idea to write a modern parody of the entire Bible—there are 66 books in the Bible, so my series will have 66 books. Maybe comic book form

Chapter 7: *Christian Children's Books*

would be good, and I could knock out one a week. I want to submit the whole series all at once. Can you suggest a market?"

Phew! I was still trying to digest his idea of rewriting the Bible. I told him as gently as possible that I couldn't think of a market offhand for such a collection, but that I was pretty sure that the Christian market should not be his starting place. But I did admire his commitment to and passion for his idea.

Writing a book, whether a board book for babies or a young adult novel, does call for commitment. Before I decide to tackle a book, I make sure I have the time and stamina it takes to write it. I also make sure I have firmly in mind my reason for writing the book. What contribution will it make to the body of Christian children's literature? Will my own faith be reflected in my work? Most importantly, I pray for guidance to God, the author of all life.

Book Ideas—Where in the World Are They?

I think every teacher has a "pet peeve" phrase that whenever uttered by students is akin to hearing fingernails scratch across a blackboard. For me, that phrase is, "I can't think of anything to write about." Huh? For anyone so afflicted, it's time to develop "Writer's Brain."

There are ideas all around us. We Christian children's writers have a head start on developing ideas into book projects, because we already have the theme that will permeate our books: Jesus is the Son of God, and He loves us.

We need to train our brains to pick up ideas from our surroundings and from the people whom we encounter each day, ideas that we can turn into a book that will sow and grow faith seeds in children.

Let me give you an example of an idea that came to me this morning while I was reading an adult Christian magazine and indulging myself with a sweet roll and bold brew at my favorite coffee shop. I was captivated by an article on an African man who started elementary school at age 84, just so he could learn to read the Bible. What an inspiring piece! I immediately thought that this man's story would make a great children's book, possibly a picture book. As soon as I got home, I scratched his name and the article reference in my notebook for further research to see if I might have a good children's book project in the making. (My writer's brain is a great idea detector, but it also forgets those ideas if I don't write them down.)

Hopefully, your visit to the children's area of a Christian bookstore has already given

Chapter 7: *Christian Children's Books*

you an idea or two. You have discovered that there are fiction and nonfiction Christian children's books. This is another decision you will have to make for your book idea—will it work best as fiction or nonfiction?

Perhaps you have a vague idea that you would like to write a book for teens encouraging celibacy until after they are married. How do you think teens would best accept this message, in a nonfiction book presenting the pros and cons of sexual restraint, or in a teen romance in which your protagonist must decide whether to give in to a boyfriend's pressure or to refuse his advances, thus jeopardizing their relationship? The teens I know would probably opt for the fiction. But this is a call you must make, before you start writing your book.

Other ideas will come to you from varying sources. Ideally, you will be in regular touch with children in your faith community. They (and your own children and neighborhood children) can be your starting place for ideas. What are their concerns? What fills them with joy? What do they like to do? Where are they in their faith lives?

Many years ago when I lived in Pittsburgh, a writer friend named Molly Wyatt told me she was appalled at the lack of table manners displayed by children she'd observed at a church supper. This made her think of other areas in which children seemed to lack social graces, such as not sending thank you notes or not answering the phone correctly. That led her to write a nonfiction Christian children's book for primary readers about manners, which she wrote in a whimsical, faith-based manner. I wish I could remember the title; I have tried to find it but can't, and Molly has since gone to be with the Lord. Still, her account of how she got a book idea is one that many of us have experienced. A need "comes to us" in the form of a book idea, we test it out to see if it's workable, and we act on that idea.

Do you keep a journal? If so, be sure to note in it any interesting bits of dialogue you overhear or scenes you observe every day. The seeds of an idea for *Yes I Can! A Kid's Guide to Dealing with Physical Challenges* came one day in the supermarket. A child noticed my prosthesis and crutches and said in a loud voice, "Look, Mommy, that lady's all broken!" I jotted down that priceless observation in my notebook and let it grow into an idea.

In this day of mainstreaming, physically handicapped children are in classrooms with non-handicapped kids. How do they handle questions, curiosity, remarks from the other children? How should they react? Will they maintain good body images even though some of their parts work differently? Will they realize that they too have been made in the image and likeness of God? I decided that Abbey Press'

Chapter 7: *Christian Children's Books*

"Elf-Help" series would be the perfect place for a book such as the one germinating in my mind. I went on their website and checked out the Elf-Help books already in print. There was none on the topic I was developing!

That is how you grow an idea. And as it sprouts, begin thinking to which age group it would most appeal and assist in their faith journeys. Then immerse yourself in reading Christian books in the same genre and for the same age group as the one you're planning. At the same time, begin your search of what has already been published and how your book will differ.

Let's go back to Molly's book on manners. Perhaps you have zeroed in on this as a theme you want to incorporate in a book, also for primary readers. First see what books are already in print on this topic, by searching *Subject Guide to Children's Books in Print* at your library. A good children's librarian can also point you to books on this topic, as can a knowledgeable salesperson at a Christian bookstore.

Also go to www.christianbooks.com, which has a huge database of Christian books in print, including children's books. I put the word "manners" in that search engine and up popped 831 Christian books on manners, many of them children's books. Yikes! That can seem discouraging, yet after reading through each of those titles, you might find a different slant for your book. Perhaps you don't see a board book listed there, yet certainly manners should begin at an early age. An idea for a board book entitled *All God's Children Are Polite!* is born.

Now you've got your idea, genre, and age target. You're committed to writing this book. You've read a bunch of Christian children's board books and have a sense of their style, length, and format. You're good to go. Say a prayer, sit down at your computer, and start typing. Some writers outline first; others go right to that all important opening line. Do what works for you.

<u>Be Ye Therefore Perfect...</u>

Yes, Jesus said this! (Matt. 5:14) As we strive for perfection in our faith journeys, it's important that this goal carry over into our writing lives. As those of you have submitted your work to publishers already know, the market is brutal, the competition fierce. The publishing world has not been immune to recent economic upheaval. Some publishers are struggling, merging, or going out of business. This, of course, also applies to the Christian publishing market. Bear in mind, too, that when a publishing staff is reduced as a cost-cutting measure, this often

Chapter 7: Christian Children's Books

requires a reduction in the number of manuscripts a publisher can review. Toward that end, many publishers have gone to a policy that requires submission through agents only. For beginning writers, this is not good news, since many literary agents will only represent writers with prior publications.

These factors, as well as honoring our God-given writing talent, make it all the more reason that we writers need to be diligent, patient, and aware of market changes and, above all, strive for perfection in our manuscripts.

In the next chapter, we will talk about writing fiction books for the Christian children's market—be prepared to get inspired!

But first, stretch yourself with the following exercise:

Writing Exercise

Create a one-to-two paragraph summary of a Christian children's book you can conceive of writing. To which age group would this book most appeal? Would it work best as fiction or nonfiction? What would be your primary reason for writing this book? (For example, goals might be one or more of the following: entertain, inform, instruct, plant faith seeds, assist readers on their faith journeys, instill morals, etc.).

For thou art my hope, O Lord God: thou art my trust from my youth.

—Ps. 71:5

Chapter 8

Sowing Truth Seeds through Fiction Books

"Why do we make a whole new deal out of writing Christian children's fiction?" a student asked recently. "Isn't it just another genre, like mystery or science fiction? Don't the same basic rules apply for writing any kind of fiction books for kids?"

My students ask really important questions! And the answer to the last one is yes, the same basic rules apply to writing Christian children's fiction books as those for writing fiction books for the secular children's market.

The difference comes in the writers' motivation, their reason for writing books. For secular authors, this is usually to inform, educate, and/or entertain their readers. For writers of Christian children's fiction, the main objective must be to show the love and mercy of Jesus Christ to their readers—in an informative, educational and/or entertaining manner. This

Sowing Seeds

objective is mirrored in the missions of publishers of Christian children's books, which often are expressed in their websites and/or guidelines.

For an example, take a look at the guidelines for Ambassador Books, Inc., a Christian publisher whose list includes adult and juvenile fiction. This publisher clearly states and differentiates its mission for each age group they target.

Fiction is a powerful vehicle for sowing faith seeds in children. Let's take a brief look at the genres of Christian children's fiction.

Genres of Fiction Books

All right, you've got the best book plot idea in the world. You are confident it will place on the bestseller list. How will it be classified? The genres of Christian children's fiction are pretty much the same as for secular children's fiction, with a couple of additions. Note that many genres combine with others, such as historical fantasy or multicultural mystery.

Adventure

These are rip-roaring, fast-paced books in which the characters are often facing danger and must rely on their cunning and survival skills. In

Chapter 8: *Fiction Books*

Christian adventure, prayer and divine intervention play a prominent role. *Isle of Swords*, a pirate story that especially appeals to intermediate readers (written by Wayne Batson, Thomas Nelson, 2007), is a good example of this genre; it also includes some fantasy.

Fantasy and Science Fiction

Even though these are separate genres (technically speaking), they have come to be considered as one, the difference being that pure science fiction has a believable scientific basis with futuristic implications. For example, a genetic mutation might be part of the plot, where a character becomes superhuman as a result. In fantasy, the magical elements introduced are most often purely a product of the writer's imagination. The battles and dragons in one Christian children's fantasy, *The Minions of Time* (Jerry B. Jenkins, Tyndale House, 2008), make it consistently a middle-grade reader favorite.

Historical Fiction

As the genre category suggests, historical fiction is set back in time. Any setting details, background events, and "real" characters included must be historically accurate, even though the protagonist and plot are usually creations of the author. Christian children's historical fiction can include stories set in biblical times.

One historical fiction book that often appears on middle school reading lists is *The Light Across the River* (Stephanie Reed, Kregel, 2008). It is set pre-Civil War and is the story of a boy helping his family to safely transport slaves to freedom via the Underground Railroad. This book is not "overtly" Christian but contains religious and faith references embraced by families in the 1830s; its message of love and tolerance reflect Christian values, hence its categorization as Christian children's fiction.

Humor

Yes, we Christians do like to laugh! Christian children enjoy rib-tickling books every bit as much as do all children. The quirky, funny *Veggie Tale* preschool series books consistently appear on the Christian Children's Books Bestseller List, maintained by and available online from the Christian Booksellers Association (CBA). One of my favorites is *God Loves You Very Much* (Cindy Kenney, ZonderKidz, 2003).

Chapter 8: *Fiction Books*

Multicultural Fiction

Christian fiction for kids featuring characters, settings, or customs/cultures of different ethnicities and/or foreign lands is highly sought and can combine with any of the other genres. Joyce Carol Thomas has written a terrific picture book entitled *Shouting!* (Hyperion, 2007) in which the "narrator" tells of her mother and other congregants dancing during their African-American church worship service.

Mystery/Suspense

This genre is one of the most popular among young readers, particularly those in primary and middle grades. Two of the many Christian children's mystery series considered "classics" and which have been reprinted several times by their publishers are *The Boxcar Children* (Albert Whitman & Company, geared toward 9-to-12-year-old readers) and *The Cul-de-sac Kids* mysteries (Baker Publishing Group, 4-to-8-year-old reading level). *The Cul-de-sac Kids* books, in particular, each teach a Bible principle, and often the characters in the stories share their love of Christ with each other. The mysteries in both series are fun for readers to try to solve. There are, of course, oodles of single titles in this genre for all age groups.

Picture Books

While Christian children's fiction picture books can be written in some of these other fiction genres, they are considered also a genre because the illustrations and text must work together to tell the story. *The Berenstein Bears and the Golden Rule* (Michael Berenstein, Stan Berenstein, and Jan Berenstein, ZonderKidz, 2008) is a good example of this genre.

Realistic/Contemporary

This is probably the largest category of Christian children's fiction books and spans all age groups, preschool through young adult.

Themes should be Christian in nature and plots include faith elements in the conflict resolution.

The nature of the conflict should be age appropriate and "universal," for example, to shoplift or not shoplift, retaliate or not, "tattle" on a sibling or keep quiet.

Checkered Flag (Chris Fabry, Tyndale House, 2008) is a terrific read for teens. The protagonists, a male and female, both high school students, must balance their Christian lives with their NASCAR dreams.

For teens/young adults, the conflict is sometimes a crisis of faith, as protagonists approach that age of liberation and are tempted to stray from the faith of their parents.

Retold and Embellished Bible Stories

As with short fiction, books that are or contain retold Bible stories are usually considered fiction since they include fictional elements; they can, for example, use animals as point-of-view characters for or to narrate the Bible stories on which they are based.

The most common retold Bible stories are for preschool and young readers and are usually in board book or picture book format, such as *Lion Misses Breakfast: Daniel and the Lions* (Tim Dowley and Steve Smallman, illustrator, Candle Books, 2004).

Embellished Bible stories are based on Bible stories but contain elements that are the product of the author's imagination, perhaps additional characters or added dialogue. A good example of this genre is *Deborah and Barak: If God Be with Us* (Trudy Morgan-Cole, Review & Herald, 2006). Although the actual Bible account of Deborah, a prophetess and only female judge of Israel, is relatively short, Morgan-Cole has built a lively plot around her and warrior Barak in which young adult readers learn what it might have been like to be a female with a prominent, authoritative position during Old Testament times.

Romance

Christian teen romances are sometimes sought by publishers. The romantic elements in plots for this readership reflect Christian values (no sex, no graphic kissing or groping scenes). Emphasis is on the male and female growing together through shared faith. A good example of this genre is *Dance and Basketball Love* by Cameron Glenn (Holy Fire Publishing, 2009).

Sports Fiction

Some publishers list books that revolve heavily around a particular sport as a separate genre. Perhaps this is because it is hoped that by so labeling a story it will appeal to boys, who are more often reluctant readers than are girls. This genre could just as easily be lumped with "realistic or contemporary" fiction. *Checkered Flag*, referenced above, would be considered sports fiction by publishers who separately categorize stories with a sports theme.

Chapter 8: *Fiction Books*

These, then, are the major genres that publishers most often use when categorizing and marketing Christian children's fiction.

Your Christian Children's Fiction Book Takes Shape

Now let's discuss the format your book will take, which will depend upon the age group you target. We'll also discuss some writing tips for each format.

Board Books

Whenever a baby is born to someone in my circle of friends and acquaintances, I race to a local Christian bookstore and buy my favorite baby gift, *Baby's First Bible* (Colin and Moira MacClean, illustrators, Standard Publishing 1996). This colorful board book, complete with plastic carrying handle, tells youngsters from their first moment of awareness that they are children of God.

Harold D. Underdown, who has edited children's books for such prestigious publishers as Charlesbridge and Orchard, maintains a wonderful website with oodles of "how-to" articles on writing for children. In his article on

Sowing Seeds

writing board books, he makes the distinction between a board book, which is actually a format, and a picture book, which he considers a genre. "What you may have done is write a picture book text that would be best published in board book format."

He suggests submitting a board book manuscript as a "picture book for the very young" and letting the publisher decide the format. His rationale is sound: board books are expensive to produce, and certainly board book texts can work as picture books instead.

However, since many publishers list these as a separate need, they will be treated separately here.

The main "readership" for board books is infants up to 2 years old, hence board books' bright colors and printing on heavy cardboard pages that are difficult for little ones to bite, tear, or otherwise demolish. Most board books are 12-to-24 pages and have extremely low word counts, sometimes as few as 50 and often no more than 200—for the entire book!

According to James Cross Giblin, award-winning children's author, board books can be the hardest for the new writer to tackle and market, since often the art work and text are submitted as a package.

Chapter 8: *Fiction Books*

<u>Writing Tips for Board Books</u>

A visiting preacher at my church told us that his grandfather gave him advice on how to be the best preacher possible: Be brief, be bright, be gone. I think these three "b's" sum up the task of a person writing a board book.

Study several before you even attempt to write your own. Make every word count. Remember what it means for the text and illustrations to work together in order to tell a complete story.

For example, let's say you are writing a book entitled "Noah Built an Ark." Your first page might read, *"Build an ark,"* God told Noah. The illustration on that and the facing page could show rain clouds on the horizon, Noah hammering boards into the ark, and curious neighbors watching.

The next page continues, God said, *"Put animals in the ark."* The illustration shows all kinds of animals going two by two up a ramp into the ark. The rain clouds are closer than in the first illustration.

Do you see what I mean? Your words are minimal but meaningful. They tell the part of the story that illustrations cannot. But without both words and illustrations, you won't really have a whole story.

Picture Books

As a general rule, fiction picture books can be roughly divided into two groups by age of listeners/readers.

The first are picture books for the younger age group, targeting 2-to-5-year-olds, which, like board books, must partner words and illustrations that result in a complete story—short word counts are best, hardly ever longer than 1000 but preferably less.

The second category of picture books targets 6-to-9-year-olds—these are usually termed "picture story books" or "story picture books" by publishers and can have longer word counts, perhaps up to 2000 words.

For the latter, illustrations are complementary in the sense that they "complete" the book; however, they are not essential to the telling of the story. The words can stand alone as a story. Still, illustrations are important for the visual pleasure of readers.

Fiction picture books make up a large body of Christian children's literature. What better way to teach about Jesus and God and faith than through visually appealing, compelling stories?

These can be written in any fiction genre. The faith element can be overt, as in retold Bible stories, or subtle, as in a story that shows a

Chapter 8: *Fiction Books*

young Christian resolving issues with a neighborhood bully by applying the biblical principle of "turning the other cheek."

Writing Tips for Picture Books

Read an armload of Christian children's fiction picture books for the age group yours will target. Note how the illustrations work with or complement the text. (Note, unless you're an accomplished artist as well as a talented writer, you don't have to do your own illustrations—a publisher will assign an illustrator after you sign a contract.) Notice the plot structure and pacing. When you begin writing your book, keep the following in mind:

- Your story must have a plot, with a beginning, middle, and ending. It must present a clear Christian message. It must feature a strong protagonist (preferably child-aged) who has an issue to resolve.

- Keep your writing lively and interesting. Use strong, active verbs. Keep adjectives and adverbs to a minimum.

- Think visually. It is difficult for an illustrator to show "thoughts." The more change of scenes in your story, the more your illustrator has to work with.

- The average picture book is 32 pages—some picture story books are 48 pages. Subtracting, say, 4 pages for "front matter" such as title and copyright pages and in some cases a couple for back matter, such as an author's note, your illustrator will have to have enough text for anywhere from 24-to-28 illustrations. To assure that you have enough, you can make yourself a "picture book dummy" by folding blank sheets of paper together to make a mock-up of how you visualize the text and illustrations together. There are several step-by-step instructive articles available online to walk you through this procedure. I've referenced one on e-How in the Bibliography.

- You can submit "notes to the illustrator" with your manuscript, but you should only do so for clarification. The illustrator will have control over the artwork. An example of a necessary note to an illustrator might be something like, (Note: Stinky Sam is a skunk).

Chapter 8: *Fiction Books*

Fiction Beginner Readers

These books are written for emerging readers and are meant for them to be able to read on their own.

Often these are sold with a "level" label, with Level 1 being for children just learning to read and containing a simply-plotted story told in short sentences and using mostly sight words—still, these children might need help from an adult to read the book.

Level 2 uses more complex sentences and is for children gaining more confidence and ability in their reading skills.

Level 3 might actually be divided into short chapters and involve a more complicated plot or even a series of short stories using the same characters.

As with all Christian children's fiction, faith and values must be an integral part of the plot(s).

Beginner readers are classified slightly differently by each publisher, so it is up to the writer to study the books of the publisher being targeted. ZonderKidz is one Christian publisher with a line of beginner readers. One of my favorites is *Sister for Sale* (Michelle Medlock Adams, ZonderKidz, 2007), which this publisher considers a Level 1 reader in its "Biblical Values, I Can Read!" series.

Writing Tips for Fiction Beginner Readers

Beginner readers should never be boring. Choose your words carefully and include strong, active words.

Where appropriate, humor is welcomed in these books.

Remember that your book will be illustrated, but unlike picture books, your words need to stand alone and result in a complete story.

Repetition works well for these readers.

God, Jesus, prayer, and/or faith values should be part of your plot.

Chapter Books

I still remember the time my next door neighbor, then seven, came running over after her first day of school, clutching a book in her hand. "Look, Miss Kathy, we got to take home a book from the school library! I got a big girl book."

Maricella had graduated from beginner readers to chapter books. This format is generally targeted at 7-to-10-year-old readers who have indeed graduated to "big girl (or boy) books."

These are usually anywhere from 6,000-12,000 words, can be written in any fiction genre, and often have just one illustration per chapter (of course, this varies).

Writing Tips for Chapter Books

Keep in mind that like Maricella, chapter book readers consider themselves "mature" and are proud of their reading ability. Never "write down" to them.

Remember that school and family and church are meaningful to these children. They are beginning to consciously develop their own identities. They are curious and eager to learn. Kids this age often begin to form attachments to fictional characters, such as those in series.

It is important to hook readers with your opening paragraph in Chapter 1. Your plot should be complex enough that you can sustain a short book length work, even having some subplots.

For example, you might be writing a contemporary fiction chapter book in which your protagonist, Josh, has moved from a suburban to an urban area. He is angry at God that he has been uprooted. No one asked him if he wanted to move! Josh is considered a "hillbilly" by his new classmates. Worse yet, the youth minister at his new church has discovered that Josh has an excellent singing voice, but the last thing Josh wants to do is to sing a solo!

You can handle a couple subplots like this, but your main "thread" will be for Josh to get over his anger at God and find a way to cope with—and eventually embrace—his new environment.

Character development is important in chapter books and novels. Readers should care about and cheer for your protagonist. Remember that none of us is "all good" or "all bad"—even the worst bully has a redeeming quality or two. Also remember that kids dislike reading about wimpy, whiny characters. Your protagonist should certainly have emotions, but not be consistently negative. Read lots of chapter books before starting yours. Appendix C lists a couple that you should be able to find at your local Christian bookstore, in your church library, or perhaps even in your public library.

Novels

The format for fiction books for middle-grade and teen readers is the novel, which can run anywhere from 15,000-40,000 words for middle graders and often 40,000-80,000 for teens, although this varies widely.

Novels are not just "long short stories." British novelist E. M. Forster defined a novel as a "fiction in prose of a certain extent." Wow, that certainly is broad! Perhaps that is because

Chapter 8: Fiction Books

so many definitions have been put forth since this literary form was first so designated in the mid-18th century.

Writing Tips for Novels

Regardless of which definition of "novel" you embrace, remember that every novel should answer these basic questions:

- What does the main character want?

- How does he or she go about getting it?

- How does achieving that quest change the main character by the end of the novel?

- In a Christian novel, the protagonist's quest should be integrally entwined with his or her Christianity.

Dr. Agatha Taormina, Professor Emeritus and Adjunct English Professor, Northern Virginia Community College, teaches that novels place more emphasis on characters than on plot, and that despite novels being fiction, they still are an accurate portrayal of the human condition.

Of course, there is an exception to every rule, and there are some novels that are plot-driven, particularly those considered "adventures."

However, in Christian novels, the emphasis is on the main character's faith journey and, consequently, even in an adventure story you will necessarily have more emphasis on your protagonist.

Writing a Christian children's novel takes commitment, a clear sense of the overall message you want your book to convey, and an ability to create a strong plot and interesting, three-dimensional characters.

Jo Louis, Editor for Christian publisher Little Lauren Books, states that the "missing" ingredient in many teen novels she sees is honesty. "Package it how you will, but honesty will best reach the audience of both nonfiction and fiction books. How can a young person relate to a character if that character can't relate to 'real life'?" She goes on to give this tip to writers: "We are looking for edgy material that may represent Scripture in a new light. God is always revealing Himself and the more time you spend with Him, the greater your understanding will be. We are not afraid of books that encompass the grace message and bring a character through addictions, etc."

Whether you are writing a middle-grade or teen/young adult Christian novel, don't send it to a publisher until you are assured of these things:

Chapter 8: *Fiction Books*

- Your plot is engaging, age appropriate, and has a Christian theme.

- Your characters are three-dimensional—readers will care about them.

- Your plot has a definite arc: a beginning, a middle that rises to a climax, and an ending that ties up all plot and subplot issues and that shows how your protagonist has changed.

- Your timeline is clear to readers throughout—when a scene is told in flashback, your readers know it is a flashback through your clear use of transitions and time markers.

  If your novel is historical fiction, be sure that any historical facts you include have been researched and are accurate.

There are, of course, other possible formats for children's fiction books, such as novelty books, comic books, pop-up books, and graphic novels. But by and large, your book will fall into one of the above formats.

So, are you itching to begin your book? Before you do, let's take a look at the other major genre in which you can write a Christian children's book, nonfiction.

But first, try your hand at the exercise for this chapter on fiction books:

Writing Exercise

Outline a Christian children's fiction book plot and determine to which age group it would most appeal. In what genre would you write it? In what format do you envision it? What faith element does your plot encompass?

For ye were sometimes darkness, but now are ye light in the Lord; walk as children of light.

—Eph. 5:8

Chapter 9
Christian Children's Nonfiction Books—Fertile Ground

Wait! Before you skip this chapter, I urge you to give me half an hour or so of your time. You see, too many writers have the same preconception of nonfiction books as do readers—they're boring, dry, hard to write. I used to think that too, early on in my writing career.

Then my editor (when I was writing for the educational market) asked me to come up with a proposal for a hi/lo (high interest, low reading level) nonfiction book, one that would deal with animals kept as pets. Whoa! Me, write a nonfiction book? What did I know about writing nonfiction? I wanted to write fiction, create my own world and characters.

But, this publisher had become overstocked with fiction and was only accepting nonfiction proposals. If I wanted a contract, I had to overcome my bias toward nonfiction. I finally came up with the idea to write a book on some of the pets that U.S. presidents had brought into the White House. Researching and writing *Presidential Pet "Tails"* (Perfection Learning, 2001) was not only a learning experience for me, it was pure joy.

Now, remember that fiction book idea you outlined at the end of Chapter 8? Before you start writing it, you might think about how it could work instead as a nonfiction book. Let's say, for example, that you decided to write a novel about a girl who feels totally lost when she first enters ninth grade. She's smaller than the other kids, has trouble making friends, and is shy. To overcome her shyness, she becomes active in her youth group, develops increased self-esteem and draws closer to Jesus when serving others.

It's a great idea, but when you play with a plot outline, it seems "lame" to you, not enough happening to write an entire book. Don't toss that idea! Consider a nonfiction book for middle-school Christians—perhaps a handbook of service project ideas. What fun that would be to write!

In Chapter 7, we discussed in general terms how to transform ideas into book proposals, but I would like to go over that in a little more depth here, since research, outlining, and organizing are such important components of writing nonfiction books. So before going into

Chapter 9: *Nonfiction Books*

the style and types of Christian children's nonfiction books, let's get specific about what you need to do before committing to writing such a book.

First Steps toward Growing Your Book

You've got your idea—now what? Let's go back to Chapter 7 and the neat idea I had one day for a nonfiction book profiling the life of the African man who started elementary school at age 84. This gentleman had a burning desire to learn so he could read the Bible, something he'd only been able to hear from missionaries during his lifetime. Certainly the Christian theme is there if your book idea comes to fruition. But first things first.

You found this idea in an article in an adult magazine. Has this fellow's story been written in a juvenile publication? Start with the Internet and put in the man's name. Let's say you find one story written about him in a Christian children's magazine that targets intermediate readers.

Your next stop is at your public library, where you search *Subject Guide to Children's Books in Print*. You find that a chapter on this man's life has been included in a teen anthology on people whose lives have made a difference.

Does this mean you shouldn't even consider writing your own children's book on this man? No!

How about writing a nonfiction Christian children's story picture book for 4-9 year old readers? Think how much young children will learn about faith and courage by reading about a man who loved Jesus so much that he risked ridicule and started school with 5- and 6-year-old children.

The next question you need to answer is, "Is there enough research material for me to access in order to write my book?" Further library and Internet research will help you decide this.

Certainly the article in which you first read about this man is one source. In that article, it indicated that many British journalists wrote articles on the gentleman's story once it was made public. You should be able to get transcripts of those articles—good! It seems like you'll have more than enough sources from which to draw information for your book.

Now is the time to make a rough outline, which confirms the fact that, yes! my idea has merit.

It is at this point that some writers of nonfiction stop and query publishers before proceeding further. A query is a letter you write to prospective publishers in which you detail your idea—summarize the book, your rationale

Chapter 9: Nonfiction Books

for thinking it will appeal to that publisher and complement its list, and, especially, why you think it will be an important addition to the world of Christian children's nonfiction. The hope is that your idea interests a publisher, and an editor responds with an encouraging, "Yes, this might be the type book we'd consider publishing. We'd be happy to look at the manuscript when it's completed." This isn't a contract or firm offer, but such a response tells the writer that there is interest in such a book. Other writers forge ahead and write their books and then try to interest publishers. Whether to query before writing or not is the writer's choice, of course.

For me, it depends upon the project. If I plan a short book such as a nonfiction picture book, I write it first because many publishers request the whole manuscript for this format rather than queries. For longer length works, it varies. But I admit that most times I do write a book before querying—it's just the way I work. My sales ability is dismal (and a query is a "sales pitch"); I was fired from my first job as a telemarketer after a week passed without my making a single sale!

A Word about Style

Christian children's nonfiction books are not textbooks. They should be interesting, informative, enlightening, inspirational—but never dull, boring, preachy, or dry.

God has blessed you with writing talent and the heart of a storyteller. Such creativity should shine through your writing.

Be sure to read several Christian children's nonfiction books in the same format as you envision yours so you can get a feel for the style and tone of these books.

Nonfiction Book Categories

To be considered a nonfiction book for Christian children, your subject must concern Christianity, Christian lifestyle, and/or the wonders of God's creation.

Because the format of nonfiction children's books depends so much on its subject matter and age of readership, the most common book types and formats will be discussed together.

These categories are by no mean exhaustive, and it seems that really creative writers are constantly coming up with new and improved book types—maybe that will be you! In the meantime, here is my categorization of Christian children's nonfiction books that reflects today's market.

Note that books on curriculum and teaching methods written for adults who work with Christian youth are not included here.

Activity Books

For the most part, activity books are for the preschool, primary, and intermediate age groups.

These can be set up in a variety of ways, but are usually not in "chapters" but rather with each activity starting on its own page.

The activities should be original (for example, perhaps one you've designed and used in a Sunday school setting), engaging, and of course centered on a Christian theme.

Activities can be for groups or individuals.

Instructions should be clear and concise, and the level of complexity designed according to the age of the children you're targeting. If adult supervision is needed for any part of the activity, be sure to note that in the activity.

A good example of this book category is *Bible Lessons in the Kitchen: Activities for Children 5 & Up* (Elaine Magee, Wiley, 1997).

Beginner Readers

As with fiction beginner readers, the nonfiction counterparts are also written to be read by a child in the early phases of developing reading skills.

Your text should be easily understood while at the same time enriching the faith of your young readers.

Topics can range anywhere from a simple account of God creating the world to a book on different types of worship.

Jesus and his Friends (part of ZonderKidz I Can Read! Beginner's Bible series, 2007) is a great example of this nonfiction category.

Bibles/Bible Studies/Bible Guides

I'm sure you're surprised to find Bibles listed here—hasn't that been "done?" Of course, and we can't improve on the original. But publishers do consider some toddler and children's bibles that have been written true to Scripture but in much more simplified language to be nonfiction—hence the listing here. Well-written children's Bible studies are often sought. These can be written for any of the age groups, including teens, and usually are based on a particular book

Chapter 9: *Nonfiction Books*

of the Bible, or perhaps might even venture into exegesis in older children's books.

The Scriptures studied should be accompanied with an application appropriate for your readership. Questions can be appended at the end of each chapter or division.

Styles and formats in this type of book vary; just be sure to be consistent.

A good primary grade Bible study book is *The First Christians: The Acts of the Apostles for Children* (Marigold Hunt, Sophia Institute Press, 2004).

Books of questions about the Bible and guides to the Bible are popular types of Christian children's nonfiction books. One that was recently released that I'd love to use with my church school students is *If I Could Ask God Anything: Awesome Bible Answers for Curious Kids* (Kathryn Slattery, Thomas Nelson Publishing, 2010).

Writing Tips for Bibles/Bible Studies/Bible Guides

Before you attempt to write a book in this category, be sure of your own Bible knowledge. Frankly, I don't recommend your trying a toddler Bible; there are so many good ones out there, and I'm not sure the market is ready for another.

For Bible studies, guides, and "questions and answer" type books, use Scripture passages you quote from the Bible version that the publisher you will target requires; if not specified, use the version you most use and be sure to indicate that version on your manuscript.

Keep your text interesting; remember, in addition to sowing faith seeds in children, your goal is to write a book that kids will read. When you look at Bible-based children's books, you'll notice the artwork is often "light," quirky, even.

Biographies

This is a huge category of Christian children's nonfiction. These can be written for children of any age and in picture book or chapter format.

They can focus on the life of anyone, living or dead, who has impacted Christianity.

Perhaps you might want to write a biography on Queen Esther or King David or another prominent Old Testament figure.

You might decide to write about Nelson Mandela, Pope Benedict, or a Christian athlete such as retired NBA star David Robinson, who has started a school for disadvantaged children and who ministers at his church.

An example of a biography of a "contemporary Christian" of interest is *Clarence*

Chapter 9: *Nonfiction Books*

Jones: Mr. Radio, a book in the young adult series *Christian Heroes: Then & Now* (Janet and Geoff Benge, YWAM Publishing, 2005).

Writing Tips for Biographies

Research, research, research. Use reliable sources. Keep notes of every source you consult. Be prepared to verify any fact you include.

For a biography to be completely nonfiction, do not add dialogue, emotions, or reactions not documented unless you do it in a speculative statement.

For example, if you write a biography on Reverend Martin Luther King, Jr., and you're recounting a particularly poignant scene, you could add something like, "How sad he must have felt!"

Include as much childhood information on your subject as you can.

If, in your research, you run across particularly good photographs of your subject, make note of where you found them so you can mention that to the publisher (if that happy time arrives and you have a contract in hand).

Write in a lively style—use your best storytelling voice.

Board Books

As described in the last chapter, board books are sturdy books targeted specifically to 0-to-2-year-old children.

Christian nonfiction books for these little ones are often elemental Bible stories and books about the Bible, bedtime prayers, simple Christian poetry, stories of the wonder of God's creation, and basic concept books (discussed in more detail below).

For example, teaching colors can be given a Christian slant; perhaps you might write a board book text showing the colors in various of God's creations, such as green grass, red roses, blue sky.

An example of a nonfiction Christian board book is *Bible Guess Who? A Slide & See Book* (Allia Zobel Nolan, Claudine Gevry, illustrator, Kregel KidZone, 2003).

Christian Living/Christian Values

Books on how to live a Christian life also make up a large portion of nonfiction books for children. These can be written on any age level and cover everything from dressing modestly to social relationships to friendship—all written to guide children and teens to understand how

Chapter 9: *Nonfiction Books*

Scripture and faith should be their "manuals" for living Godly lives.

A good example of a Christian living book is *A Teen's Guide to Christian Living: Practical Answers to Tough Questions about God and Faith* (Bettie Youngs, Jennifer Leigh Youngs, and Debbie Thurman, Faith Communications, 2003).

Writing Tips for Christian Living/Christian Values Nonfiction Books

Lively, nonjudgmental, non-preachy style is key to writing successful books in this category. Involve your readers. Use anecdotes. Pose questions. Know your audience and address situations and issues that you know are important for these children.

Look at what's already been published in Christian living books for the age group you're targeting. How will your book differ?

Be current. Don't write a chapter on how to answer the telephone. Now, texting—that might be an issue to consider.

Sowing Seeds

Christianity/Theology/Church History

This category of nonfiction books for Christian children is perhaps the most difficult to write unless you have a strong background yourself in the history and roots of Christianity and in theology in general.

Even if you write a 75-word nonfiction board book teaching who Jesus is, it must be theologically sound.

I know there is a fine line here on what might be considered fiction and what would be considered nonfiction. Here is an example that I hope will clarify this a bit—note, too, that a publisher would make the final determination, but it is helpful for the writer to have an idea of genre. When reading publisher guidelines; you will find many that accept, say, only nonfiction.

Nonfiction board book text:
>Jesus loves children.
>Jesus loves poor people.
>Jesus loves people of every color.
>Jesus loves everyone!

Fiction board book text:
>Jesus loved children.
>"Come, let's play a game," Jesus said one day.
>So Jesus gathered the children around him.

Chapter 9: Nonfiction Books

Note that the first example is a simplification of what we're told in Scripture about Jesus.

The second certainly revolves around a biblical truth, but the addition of the dialogue and scene not in Scripture is the author's way of showing little children Jesus' love for them—but it would be considered fiction.

Subject matter for this category is vast! It goes without saying that the level on which you write depends upon the age group you are targeting.

As you write, let the Bible be your main source. Keep your topic narrowly focused.

For example, you might decide to write a book for middle-grade readers on how the Gospels came to be, or a book for primary-grade readers on the roots of the early church.

Research is vital. If you write a book in this category, I urge you to have a minister or credentialed theologian review it for you to ensure its accuracy. Mention in your cover or query letter to a publisher that you have done this.

A terrific theological book written for 9-to-12-year-old Christians is *Jesus Is Alive!: Evidence for the Resurrection, Children's Edition* by Josh and Sean McDowell (Regal, 2009).

Another, targeted at 4-to-8-year-old readers, is *Fact or Fantasy: A Study in Chris-*

tian Apologetics for Children (David Walters, Good News Fellowship Ministry, 1991).

Writing Tips for Christianity/Theology/Church History

Remember to keep readers involved! The best way to do this is to periodically address readers directly.

Let's say you want to write a book you've tentatively titled *What Does Jesus Look Like?* You envision it as a picture book for 4-to-6-year-old children. Following is an example of one way you might open that would include readers:

> What do you think Jesus looks like? Do you picture him tall or short, with straight black hair or curly brown hair? Are his eyes blue as the sky or dark as night? Do you see him wearing blue jeans or dress pants, tennis shoes or flip-flops?
>
> What do you think Jesus looks like? The answer is that we don't know. When Jesus lived on Earth, there were no cameras. We do not have a photo of him. We won't know what he looks like now until we meet him in heaven. But from reading the Bible and studying his-

Chapter 9: *Nonfiction Books*

tory, we can know some things that give us clues about how he might have looked.

Then you could proceed to present some information about the part of the world where Jesus was born and lived, traditional dress for boys and men, and customs and daily living during Jesus' time on Earth, including the fact that there were no barber shops and that many men had beards, etc.

Of course, while researching your book, make notes of Scriptures and other sources on which you're basing the information you present.

Concept Books

Books in this category are generally for preschoolers or kids in kindergarten or first grade.

They can be instructive in basic tools that are new to these children, such as the alphabet, numbers, colors and shapes. A Christian concept book might be something like "Bible ABCs."

Concept books also address more abstract ideas such as feelings, or what it means to "walk with Jesus." *Where Is God When I'm Scared?* (Veggie Tales Board Book by Cindy

Kenney, ZonderKidz, 2004) and *If Jesus Walked Beside Me* (Jill Roman Lord, Renee Graaf , illustrator, also a board book, Candy Cane Press, 2006) are good examples of Christian children's concept books.

Writing Tips for Concept Books

Note that because concept books are generally for the youngest readership, often fiction techniques/storytelling styles are employed. These might be considered fiction by some publishers, nonfiction with fiction techniques by others. You need only look at a publisher's catalogue to see whether or not it publishes books such as yours, regardless of how it's classified.

Craft Books

Kids love to make things, whether in a group setting such as vacation Bible school or Sunday school or at home.

In the Christian marketplace, craft books should contain ideas for crafts with a Christian theme and/or celebrate God's creation. These can specialize in just one art (for example, 50 Bible character finger puppets you can make), or can be a compilation of several different types of crafts, such as *Big Book of Christian Crafts* by Katy Ross (Millbrook Press, 2002), written for 4-to-8-year-old readers.

Writing Tips for Craft Books

Instructions should be clear and concise, with materials needed being easily attainable in most households or classrooms.

Crafts that recycle such things as plastic water bottles are super, because they contain "teachable moments" about being good stewards of God's earth.

Study what's already out there and see if you can find a niche, such as a book of simple crafts like Scripture bookmarks that can be given as gifts to residents in a local nursing home.

Devotional/Meditation Books

This category of Christian children's books is generally targeted to intermediate and teen readers.

Very often they target one gender or the other.

The length of these books depends on the number of devotions contained. Sometimes there is one for each day of the year. Each devotion is usually set up the same way, the most usual format being a Scripture selection followed by the devotion followed by a prayer or application based on the Scripture and devotion.

Sometimes these books are combined with journals (discussed below). *Me, Myself and I: Youth Meditations for Grades 5-8* (Sandra McLeod Humphery, CSS Publishing Company, 2008) and *The One Year book of Devotions for Girls* (Tyndale Children's Bible Hour, 2000) are examples of popular devotionals.

Writing Tips for Devotionals/Meditation Books

This is a hard market to break into because there are so many good devotionals out there. Here's where your writer's brain needs to kick into high gear.

Find a "niche" market, for example, "devotions for kids who have physical challenges" or, if you're really brave, perhaps you can start a whole new fad with something like, "101 devotions to text to your friends" (you could put the title in "text" if you're familiar—I've yet to text anyone!).

If you compile devotions into a book and you include some you've had published previously, such as in a Christian children's magazine, be sure you own the rights or can get permission to use the devotion(s) if you do not own the rights.

Drama/Plays

While more often than not this is a fiction category, some plays and skits such as Passion plays can be written true to Scripture and thus be considered nonfiction. Steven James' *24 Tandem Bible Hero Story Scripts for Children's Ministry* (Standard Publishing, 2004) is in the nonfiction children's section at Christian bookstores.

History

There are some books written for Christian children that contain history other than church or Bible history. This is not a large body of work, but you might have just such a book in mind—perhaps you can conceive of a story picture book about the faith of the Puritans and how they practiced it upon settling on Plymouth Rock.

A good example of this genre is *From Sea to Shining Sea for Children: Discovering*

God's Plan for America in Her First Half-Century of Independence, 1787-1837 (phew, that's a mouthful!) by David Manuel, Peter Marshall, and Anna Wilson Fishell (Revell, 1993), written for 9-to-12-year-old readers.

Writing Tips for History

In addition to impeccable research, writers need to be very organized and structure these books in a chronological manner. Timelines are helpful. A storytelling voice is crucial.

Journals

This is a popular format for Christian children, particularly middle-grade and teen readers. Often these are combined with devotionals, or perhaps each page starts with a Scripture and a writing prompt.

There is a wide variety of structures, and there is room for an inventive writer to come up with yet another, targeted to specific subsets of readers.

Be sure to study what's out there, and see if you can come up with your own idea. Kids love this interactive format, where they can examine their own ideas of faith and life in private.

Two journals that I often give as gifts are *Who Am I? A Journal for Answering the Question, Who Am I?* (Matthew Price and Joe Anderson, Howard Books, 2004), written for 9- to-12-year-olds, and *God's Little Devotional Journal for Teens* (Henry Drummond, Honor Books, 2001).

Picture Books

Nonfiction picture books can be written in almost any of the nonfiction genres presented here; I'm including it as a separate entry just to remind you that format is key when structuring your text.

Remember that you will have a partner, your illustrator.

Think visually and keep your writing lively.

I love Julie Cantrell's book, *God Is with Me through the Day* (ZonderKidz, 2009).

As with fiction picture books, standard nonfiction picture books are generally 32 pages, so bear that in mind as you plan for about 28 pages of text/illustrations combined.

Poetry

Your visit to the Christian bookstore most likely showed you that there are some neat books of Christian children's poetry, particularly for the preschool, primary, and middle-grade readers.

A good example is *Zack, You're Acting Zany! Playful Poems and Riveting Rhymes* (Marty Nystrom and Steve Bjorkman, "Bible Characters in Rhyme" series, Standard Publishing, 2010). This book is a fun way to introduce Bible characters to children—and they will remember them!

Writing Tips for Poetry

Unless you are an accomplished poet, don't try writing in this genre! The most common reason books of children's rhymes or poetry are rejected is due to poor rhythm and rhyme (90% is dreadful, according to an editor friend of mine who wishes to remain anonymous!).

Prayer Books

These books, often for younger Christian children, are collections of original prayers, usually illustrated, to introduce children to prayer

Chapter 9: Nonfiction Books

as a way they can communicate with the Lord. Often these prayers are also poems.

An example of this genre is *A Child's First Book of Prayers* by Lois Rock and Allison Jay (Augsburg Fortress Publishers, 2002), which is targeted to 4-to-8-year-olds.

Puzzle and Word Game Books

These books contain collections of puzzles and word games such as those we discussed in Chapter 6 which appear in Christian children's magazines.

Often the books contain just one type puzzle, such as Ken Save's *Super Bible Word Searches* (Barbour Publishing, 2000), designed for 4-to-8-year-old children.

Writing Tips for Puzzle and Word Game Books

If you compile a book such as this and include some puzzles or games that you've previously published in, say, a Christian children's magazine, be sure the rights have reverted back to you, or that you get permission to use those puzzles/games in your book.

Self-Help Books

Just as do adults, children can benefit greatly from self-help books. They love to be able to resolve their own issues! Christian self-help books include advice to make children proactive in everything from death of a parent to dealing with bullies. In addition to furnishing readers with practical coping strategies, it is the job of the author to stress prayer and Jesus as ever-present sources of support.

A good example of this genre (I humbly assert) is my latest book, *Yes I Can! A Kid's Guide to Dealing with Physical Challenges* (illustrated by R.W. Alley, Abbey Press, 2010). It is a nonfiction picture book and part of Abbey Press' "Elf Help" series.

Writing Tips for Self-Help Books

Be certain that you have knowledge or experience in the subject matter before attempting to give self-help advice. If you're writing a book for Christian teens on dealing with depression, and if you're not a mental health professional, make sure you consult with one. A "smile, pray, and be happy" solution may be detrimental to a reader seeking help other than platitudes.

Chapter 9: *Nonfiction Books*

Teen/Young Adult Nonfiction Books

Most of the genres above can be written for a teen audience. I have listed this as a separate category, too, because it is so important that writers for this age group be in touch with teens and their issues.

Think back to when you were a teen, trying to wrap your mind around a zillion things at once—body changes, sexual awareness, peer pressure, preparing for college or the work world, relationships, and, yes, faith issues. As teens approach 18 and are about to be liberated, their Christianity is often called into question, by themselves and others.

I don't know about you, but I'm glad I'm not a teen in today's world, where drug use and flaunting one's sexuality are the norm. During my teen years, I never heard of date rape drugs. I don't remember any of my friends in high school having eating disorders, or getting pregnant. These are the type social issues that need to be addressed in nonfiction literature for Christian teens today. It takes a special writer with strong faith and insight, as well as a sensitive nature, to write for this age group. Maybe that's you! What a terrific, specialized ministry.

Since its release in 2008, the young adult book, *Do Hard Things: A Teenage Rebellion Against Low Expectations* (Alex and Brett Harris, Chuck Norris, Multnomah), has been at or close to the top of the best-selling Christian children's books list, published by the Christian Booksellers Association. If you go on Amazon.com and read the reviews for this book, they will lift your heart—most are written by teens, who point to the positive influence this book has had on their lives. As an author, when readers give such testimony after reading something I've written, I know I've done my job of ministering through the written word.

<u>Writing Tips for Teen/Young Adult Nonfiction Books</u>

I can only repeat—know your audience! If you're not in touch with the world of teens, don't try to write for them.

Oh my goodness, I believe this chapter is finally drawing to a close. I hope it has inspired you to at least prayerfully consider writing some nonfiction books for Christian children. Next, as we begin to wind down our journey together, we'll look at the nuts and bolts of sending out your manuscripts.

But first, wrap up this chapter with an exercise:

Chapter 9: *Nonfiction Books*

> ## *Writing Exercise*
> Write a paragraph or two summarizing a nonfiction book for Christian children that you would find interesting to write and research. What is your purpose in writing this book? Which age group would your book target? What impact do you expect it would have on your readers?

O God, thou hast taught me from my youth,
and hitherto have I declared
thy wondrous works.

—Ps. 71:17

Chapter 10
Sealed with a Prayer—Sending Off Your Manuscripts

Imagine...you're an editorial assistant, working for a popular Christian children's book publisher. It's Monday morning, you've just left a staff prayer meeting to start the week, and you carry your coffee to your desk, which is barely visible beneath stacks of unopened manuscript envelopes. You're still pumped from the prayer session...*Maybe this will be the day I find that jewel, that manuscript that shouts "bestseller,"* you think as you slit open the first envelope. The contents are handwritten on yellow-lined paper; you search in vain for the required self-addressed, stamped envelope (S.A.S.E.). You toss the manuscript into your blue "to be recycled" wastebasket and move on to the next envelope. It's thick as a phone book—obviously the writer did not read your publisher's guidelines that clearly stipulate, "Queries and first chapters only." At least there is an S.A.S.E., so you clip a form reject to the massive manuscript, slip it in your outbox, and reach for the next envelope...

Put Your Best Manuscript Forward

Ask any editor! The scenario described above is more the rule than the exception. While we writers decry slow publisher responses and those cold, form rejects, editorial staffs wrestle daily with stacks of unsolicited manuscripts (dubbed the "slush pile"), looking for those precious few which are professionally prepared and conform to the publisher's guidelines. From that small number, a staff member, usually an editorial assistant, will assess the manuscripts for subject/theme suitability. This is the next step in narrowing the pool of "possibilities."

If the publisher does not publish fiction, fiction manuscripts are returned to their authors. If the publisher is denominational, say, Methodist, a picture book on a child preparing for the sacrament of "first confession," a Catholic rite, will be rejected no matter how well-written.

By day's end, our frazzled editorial assistant may have one or two manuscripts deemed suitable to send up the editorial ladder. You want yours to be one of them.

Chapter 10: *Sending Off Your Manuscripts*

Preparation

Whether your targeted publisher requests mail or electronic submissions, your manuscript needs to be as perfect as you can make it. Proofread the entire manuscript or manuscript portion that you're submitting before you send it off, regardless of how many people have proofed it for you. I guarantee you'll find an error or two.

Next, be certain that your manuscript is in professional format, typed in a basic font such as Times New Roman, type size 12—double spaced, at least one inch margins all around, pages numbered.

Don't forget page headers. If your manuscript pages become separated on a busy editor's desk—and they will, odds are that those without page headers will not make it back into the manuscript from whence it came. My page headers after page 1 (which includes full information—my name, address, phone, email) are simple: Manuscript title—Muldoon.

If you are mailing your manuscript, be certain to print it on good stock (20 lb), and check each page to ensure that it printed well.

If you are attaching your manuscript to an email cover letter, be sure that you have saved it in an easily accessible program—usually Microsoft Word. I believe there is a version of Word that works on Macs, too.

But wait! Before you hit "send" or seal that envelope, go back and review what the publisher you've targeted wants you to send. If you are asked for "complete" manuscripts, then prepare a brief cover letter to which you will attach the manuscript. Here is a sample:

Sample Cover Letter for Manuscript

(My street address)

(Date)

(Editor's name)
(Publication name)
(Publisher's address)

Dear (Editor's name):

Jesse Santos is determined to land the role of Prince Charming in his school play despite his cerebral palsy—and the discouragement of his siblings.

"Why Not Jesse?" is a 582-word story targeted to your 7-to-9-year-old readers. I am submitting it for consideration for the September 2007 issue of (Publication name) with the theme of "determination."

Thank you for considering my story, which I have attached, as well as an SASE. I look forward to hearing from you.

Sincerely,

Chapter 10: *Sending Off Your Manuscripts*

Kathleen Muldoon

Enc.: Manuscript
      S.A.S.E.

Sample Query Letter

Perhaps the publisher you're targeting requests a query letter. As we discussed earlier, these are longer because you are hoping that it will result in an invitation to send in your manuscript. Here is the body of a query letter I sent last year to the editor of a themed children's magazine—of course it was formatted as a business letter, as above:

RE: Query for (name of publication) Jul/Aug 2010 issue, "Spies & Spying"

What a great theme! I think your readers may enjoy reading about spies their own age, and there have been several throughout history. My favorite is John Darragh, 14-year-old son of famed Revolutionary Lydia Darragh. He and his parents spied on the British soldiers, who had taken over a room in the Darragh home in Philadelphia, Pennsylvania. Whenever they overheard battle plans that would affect the Continental Army, Mr. Darragh coded the information on a scrap of paper, Mrs. Darragh sewed it into buttons on John's coat, and he transported the message to his brother, a soldier, in the encampment in the woods on the periphery of the city. His brother would then cut off the buttons and get them to General George Washington.

I would like to write John's story (tentatively titled "Spy Buttons") in a 400-word article, using fiction techniques. I would focus it on one mission of John's, showing the dangers he faced as he was stopped and searched along the way. I plan to include dialogue, which would be supplied by me, unless this would not be acceptable to you. Per your guidelines, attached is a partial bibliography I would use; most documents I found focused on Lydia Darragh but included John's story. The two books focus on John.

Thank you for considering my idea. I can have the article to you within two weeks of notification, should you select it.

Since this was emailed, there was no need for an S.A.S.E.

For book manuscripts, those that are mailed or emailed to publishers requesting "complete manuscripts" need only a cover letter.

Sample Query Letter with Outline and First Three Chapters

If a publisher specifies, say, a query with an outline and the first three chapters, the body of your letter might look like this:

Chapter 10: *Sending Off Your Manuscripts*

I was delighted to read in the March/April SCBWI Bulletin that (name of publisher) is launching a new line of chapter books, focusing on contemporary children struggling to be good Christians in school and at home. What a terrific ministry this will be for these eager young readers who are just beginning to understand the relationship between their actions and their faith. I recently completed writing a chapter book for Christian children that I believe will be a good fit for your list.

When Mrs. Mularkey Came is a 9500 word chapter book for 7-to-9-year-old readers in which Brad Morris and his third grade classmates are devastated when their teacher is sent overseas with her military reserve unit to serve a one year term of duty—right in the middle of the school year. Now, in addition to dealing with his parents' divorce, his anger at God, and the nasty Alanna May who sits in front of him in class, Brad agonizes over the new teacher due to arrive after winter break. Will she accept the fact that the only way he can contain his anger is by refusing to speak? Enter the quirky, flamboyant Mrs. Mularkey, who soon has the class under her spell—and Brad out of his shell.

Per your guidelines, I have attached an outline of my book as well as the first three chapters. Also attached are a list of my previous publications and an S.A.S.E. Thank you for considering this query. Upon your request, I would be delighted to send the rest of this manuscript. I look forward to hearing from you.

Note that in a query letter such as the above, you don't need to do as much "selling" because you are attaching a couple chapters, and the editor can tell from those whether or not your book might be a good match for that publisher.

Sowing Seeds

Sample Query Letter for Book

If you're sending a book query only, it should contain a little more information:

Saint Kevin is one of Ireland's most beloved saints. Almost all of the many legends surrounding his life focus on the animals which he loved and which, in turn, loved him. The most common, of course, is the tale of Saint Kevin and King O'Toole's goose. I chose to focus my story picture book text on two miracles involving an otter. I believe that young readers will be enchanted by this gentle man and the otter that first saved his prayer book and later the entire community of Kevin's monks.

I'm delighted with the recent surge in interest in all things Celtic, but in particular for the Celtic saints. I have a vast collection of books on these holy men from which I was able to draw most of my information, and I also was blessed to be able to e-mail chat with Father Timothy Joyce, an abbot and author of one of the best books on the Celtic monasteries and saints.

If you would like to see this manuscript, *Saint Kevin and the Otter*, I will be pleased to send it to you. Its total length is 1850 words and includes an author's note in the back matter that contains some basic information on how the Celtic saints' legends originated in the oral tradition, and how they came to be recorded and saved.

I am an instructor for the Institute of Children's Literature and have authored several books in the

Chapter 10: Sending Off Your Manuscripts

educational markets as well as two saints' biography books for (name of publisher).

I am attaching an SASE. Thank you for taking the time to review this query. I look forward to hearing from you.

If you're submitting your manuscript to a denominational publisher, be sure to indicate somewhere in your cover letter that you are either a member of that denomination or that you have researched the beliefs of that denomination.

If you have special credentials that boost your credibility as author of the manuscript you're submitting, include these in your cover or query letter. For example, if you're submitting a proposal for a nonfiction book for Christian teens, your work as a teen mentor or youth group leader is a good credential to mention.

Summaries

If you are asked to include a summary of your book, this can be single-spaced. Try to keep the summary to one page.

It should be a concise plot summary if fiction, including a paragraph on the beginning, another on the middle and climax, and a final one on the conclusion.

If nonfiction, your summary should give a capsule overview of the topic your book covers. Picture the summary you write as being on the book jacket, and endeavor to give it the "essence" of your book.

Bibliographies

If your query or manuscript is to be accompanied by a bibliography, this should be prepared in one of the many acceptable bibliography formats. Pick one and stick to it—be consistent. Be sure to enter your electronic sources, as well. College handbooks, some grammar books and dictionaries, and style books such as *The Christian Writer's Manual of Style* will show you how to prepare a bibliography.

Outlines

If a publisher requests an outline with your query, do not panic! For nonfiction, you can use a standard outline format such as the one you learned when you wrote your first high school term paper; or, you can do a summary or narrative outline, such as:

Chapter 1. Introduces the Gospel of Mark, including when it was most likely written and by

Chapter 10: *Sending Off Your Manuscripts*

whom. Presents one of themes: Jesus is presented as a man of action and authority...

Narrative chapter outlines work particularly well for fiction.

S.A.S.E.s

Just a word about S.A.S.E.s—be certain these include enough postage to return the manuscript to you. If they do not, your manuscripts are discarded. The exception to this is when you are submitting to publishers that clearly state in their manuscripts that they reply only if interested. This means that they discard manuscripts that do not interest them, so there is no need to include the S.A.S.E.

A Word About Copyrighting

One of the most difficult steps of the submission process for many of my students is actually sending out their work. "What if someone steals my work, my ideas?" and "Should I copyright my manuscript before I send it?" are probably two of the most common questions I'm asked.

There are entire books written on copyright law, and I won't even attempt to summarize that law here.

The answer to the second question, provided by the Children's Book Council, and one by which I abide, is: "It is not necessary to copyright a manuscript if you are sending it to a reputable publisher...Legally, your manuscript is automatically copyrighted the moment you create it."

Certainly if you want to register your copyright, you can find out how to do this through the Library of Congress U.S. Copyright Office at www.copyright.gov. I have never done this prior to submitting a manuscript, nor have I ever had a manuscript "stolen."

Note that "ideas" cannot be copyrighted. Magazines copyright their publications; whether or not the rights revert back to you after publication depends upon the contract you signed.

Book publishers will spell out in their contracts whether or not it is their responsibility or the author's to register copyrights.

A Word about Literary Agents

Another frequently-asked question from my students is, "Do I need an agent?" Certainly agents are nice to have, and there are publishers that will only accept manuscripts submitted through agents (these are book publishers; you seldom if ever submit material to magazines via an agent).

Chapter 10: *Sending Off Your Manuscripts*

Perhaps a better question to ask is, "Can I get an agent?" The answer most often is "no," at least not right away, probably not until you have some publishing credits. But if you want to try to procure representation, start with Sally E. Stuart's listing of literary agents in her annual *Christian Writers' Market Guide*; you should then go online and find out what the agent requires—they set forth guidelines just as publishers do as to what you should submit.

Keeping Track

Be sure you keep good records of when you send out your manuscripts and to whom you've sent them.

Being technologically challenged, I use an old-fashioned index card system, one card for each manuscript. I note the manuscript title, genre, and word count on the top line, as well as the postage cost (including S.A.S.E.) for tax purposes. The lines below are my tracking information in four columns: Date sent, Publisher, Estimated Response Time, Response.

My technologically astute writer friends have developed spread sheets to keep track of their manuscripts. Others use a notebook system. Devise a tracking system that works for you.

Once a month I go through my index cards to see if I have manuscripts on which I have to follow up with a status query to the publisher.

Self-Publishing—Another Option

Many books on writing don't mention the self-publishing industry, perhaps because in days of old it was viewed as somewhat disreputable. Its label of "vanity publishing" also cast aspersions on self-published writers, who were perceived as being unable to make it in the "real publishing world."

Today, the various self-publishing avenues are a viable and, in some cases, needed alternative to traditional publishing. Most self-publishing companies are not only reputable, but for many writers they are preferable.

Even some traditional publishers have gone to a "co-venture" publishing model, meaning that authors and publishers share some of the publishing expenses.

One Rationale for Exploring the World of Self-Publishing

Having never researched nor been published through this expanding industry, myself, I've

Chapter 10: Sending Off Your Manuscripts

asked John Evans, a preacher for the church of Christ and author of award-winning *How to Study the Bible: A Discussion and Workbook in 12 Lessons* (Outskirts Press, 2008), to share with you his knowledge of and experience with this part of the publishing industry.

"As a full-time minister of the gospel, I often write Bible study workbooks to help with my teaching," Evans says. "For years, I printed these booklets at a local quick-copy shop but ran into problems when people would ask for additional copies. It was too much work and expense to have just one or two copies printed and bound at a time."

"To solve this problem, I began researching a variety of self-publishing options which would allow others to order my workbooks whenever they needed them. My goal was to make the material easily available, in an attractive format, to those who wanted it."

Evans discovered that there are many choices available to those thinking about self-publishing their work.

Three Self-Publishing Options

"One option," he reports, "is to go to a standard book printer who will print X number of copies for X number of dollars. You write a check and receive a box of books professionally printed to your specifications."

"Typesetting, art work, size, paper type, and so forth are negotiated with the printer.

"Typically, the greater the number of books you order, the lower the price per book, but the higher the total cost.

"Books printed this way are often warehoused by the author and offered through whatever channels the author has access to.

"A second option is to go a POD (print-on-demand) publisher, who performs a variety of services for different fees. Many times these publishers will submit your title for sale through the major online bookstores. POD technology allows your book to be printed and published one-at-a-time. The book exists as a computer file until somebody orders a copy.

"Services, prices, and contracts vary widely from publisher to publisher.

"Any kind of color printing (except for the cover) can result in a very expensive book.

"Usually the author can order copies of his own work at a discounted price.

"Electronic books (eBooks) are a third, less-common, option. Many POD publishers can offer an eBook version of your work—often for a fee—in conjunction with the paper copy. A few publishers offer eBooks only."

Chapter 10: *Sending Off Your Manuscripts*

Before You Decide...

"Authors should ask and answer a number of important questions before pursuing a self-publishing option," Evans continues. "What will my budget stand? Generally, the more services you require, the more you pay.

"All manuscripts need to be professionally proofread and edited. Good cover work is a must. Do you have qualified friend who can help, or will you need to hire these services?

"How will your books be distributed? Do you require only a few copies for friends and family, or is the book meant for wider distribution? How will you reach your intended audience?

"Does your book require color graphics, which may be too expensive with current print-on-demand technology?

"What rights will you keep with the options you're considering?

"Self-publishers often fall short in three areas: covers are often poorly designed; proofreading and editing are sloppy or nonexistent; and, the list price is too high! POD books, because of the technology involved and the built-in fees of many companies, are often too expensive for the average customer. An unknown author with expensive books usually sells few copies. I've learned to find ways to keep my own prices under $10 per copy for my workbooks, which helps attract potential readers. I'd rather make less money per book, yet get more books into the hands of my intended audience. Covers should look professional, not like cookie-cutter templates. Also, readers notice sloppy editing instantly. Make your manuscript the best it can be before you publish it.

"Read the contract! Know what rights you're keeping and which ones you're signing away. Study the book pricing and discount rates carefully. Remember that many POD publishers will try to up-sell you on services you may not require. Remember your budget and stick to it."

You, A Salesperson?

With traditional publishing, the bulk of marketing and promotion of your book often falls to the publisher. If you self-publish your book, this largely becomes your responsibility.

"Marketing and self-promotion are extremely important if you expect your work to receive distribution beyond friends and family," Evans advises. "If you want your book to reach its intended audience, you have to find a way to get as many sample copies as possible into the hands of typical readers. Few self-published books sell unless the author is willing to advance and advertise his own work. Marketing and promoting do not magically happen!"

Chapter 10: Sending Off Your Manuscripts

Self-publishing is not for every author, but there are many who have been highly successful and whose books, like John Evans', have won awards. "Keep realistic expectations," he advises. "Yes, you've worked hard on your book, but that does not guarantee a best-seller. Self-publishing is a marathon, not a sprint. Consistent effort, over time, yields results."

In Chapter 11, we'll examine the type of responses you may get to your manuscript submissions to the traditional publishing market.

But first, let's wrap up this chapter with an exercise:

Writing Exercise

Choose a current Christian book publisher and read its submission guidelines. With either a completed manuscript, a work in progress, or an envisioned book manuscript in mind, draft a letter to that publisher that conforms to its guidelines. For example, if the publisher wants a query with an outline and bibliography, draft your letter as a query and indicate you've attached what the publisher specifies. Show in your letter that you "know" that publisher's list and indicate why your book would be a good match for the publisher.

Ye are all the children of light,
and the children of the day;
we are not of the night, nor of darkness.

—1 Thess. 5:5

Chapter 11
Blessed Are They Who Wait on the Lord—and on Publishers

I vividly remember the first time I sent out a short story manuscript to a small Christian magazine which stated a six-to-eight-week response time. Like a child beginning a countdown to her birthday, I "x'd" out days on my calendar until I reached the end of the eighth week. Despite my prayer pleas and daily ambushing our postman, I had no response from the publisher.

I sent off a brief status query letter, just like I'd learned to do in a "marketing your manuscripts" seminar, and again began a fruitless wait.

Another month passed before I sent a second query, this time still polite but with "second status request" on top, in bold type and underlined.

When that failed to bring a response, I committed the ultimate "no-no"; I called the publisher, was transferred to an assistant editor's voicemail, and left a message. I never received a response to that message.

Three months after that phone call, the postman delivered what I recognized as my S.A.S.E. I ripped it open and found an "accept" letter inside. On the bottom, a kindly editor had taken the time to write by hand, "Sorry for the late response. Sometimes a delay is profitable, however. Good things often come to those who wait." Indeed! I have never again heckled a publisher. A less patient editor than this one may have tired of my pestering, clipped a form reject to my manuscript, and sent it back to me.

With an increasing number of publishers accepting email queries and manuscript submissions, response times have been reduced. But the range of responses remains pretty much the same. So, let's talk about these, from the least desirable to the ultimate, a contract!

No Response

"I'd rather get a reject than no response," grumbled a student. I agree, of course. It's frustrating when it seems that your query or manuscript is either lost in cyberspace or floating around the post office, perhaps tossed in an "undeliverable" box.

Follow-up status queries might result in a "we never received your manuscript—feel free to submit it again" (do so, if you want to try again) or, again, no response.

If I get no response to a status query after waiting a reasonable period of time (for me, that's about three months), I then send a short, polite note withdrawing my manuscript from consideration. Whether or not you do this should depend on how badly you want your manuscript published by that publisher. You can continue with the status queries, but, alas, these are often fruitless. Usually, it's best to move on and try another publisher.

The "R" Word

I've often thought that it would be really cool to be editor for a book containing unique rejects, submitted by their recipients. But then I figured that would be one book manuscript that would surely be rejected.

Still, there are many types of rejects, some less irritating and more original than others. One of my favorites of the many I've received begins with, "I hate rejects, don't you?" followed by a cartoon of a pathetic-looking, harassed editor. Let's look at a few of the more common rejects we writers must steel ourselves to receive.

The Hated Form Reject

These are the ones that may or may not be dated or include the name of your manuscript, followed by a Dear Author: We can't use your manuscript for the following reason(s)...This is followed by a list of possible reasons, one or more of which might be checked. The most commonly checked is the very vague, "Doesn't suit our current needs." Huh? Does that mean it might suit their needs at a later date? Should you wait and try again? I wouldn't. This is a "catchall" phrase which you should probably consider a "not interested" and move on to another market. Then there are those one-line rejects that don't even have a checklist!

Flattering Rejects

I put these right after form rejects because, while an editor took the time to write a brief letter, it doesn't tell you anything. These often begin, "I really enjoyed reading your chapter book..." and end with, "Unfortunately, it doesn't suit our list. We wish you luck placing it elsewhere." The problem I have with these is that I study the

Chapter 11: *Watt on Publishers*

guidelines and book catalogs of any publisher before I submit my work, and I've chosen that publisher precisely because I feel my work *will* suit their list. I generally will not submit another manuscript to that publisher because now I don't feel as though I know what they want.

Form Reject with a Note

If an editorial staff member takes the time to write a note, however brief, on the bottom of your reject, take heart! I recently had one on which the note read, "Loved your story but we recently published one with the same theme." God bless editors who take the time to take the sting out of rejection by giving a bit further explanation which implies that, "Your writing is good, we just can't use this particular story." I'd send that story to another publisher, but would also send a different manuscript to the editor who wrote that note, making sure, of course, that it suits his or her publication.

Encouraging Rejects

Much like the form rejects with a note, these are instead letters which, although stating that the particular manuscript cannot be used and explaining why, encourage you to submit something else. Hooray! If you get such an invitation, follow up with a suitable manuscript, and send it with a cover letter to the editor who wrote the letter. Start it with something like,

Dear Ms. Smith,

Thank you for your letter of May 2. Per your invitation, I am submitting another picture book manuscript titled *Can Jesus Hear My Prayers?*...

Keep 'Em Circulating

After you get a reject, allow yourself about five minutes to gnash your teeth and stomp your foot, then get over it.

Despite the stated reason, if any, rejection can mean anything from "we're overstocked with manuscripts" to "we're considering folding and are not purchasing manuscripts at this time" to "you're writing is not up to par" or "your market targeting needs work."

First, ensure yourself that neither of the last two reasons is valid—you know your manuscript is well-written and that you've submitted it to a publisher whose guidelines seemed in line with your theme or topic.

If you think perhaps your manuscript does need to be polished, polish it; if you feel you need to rethink your market choice, rethink.

Chapter 11: Wait on Publishers

Then send your manuscript to another suitable market. Keep your manuscripts circulating.

Definite Maybes

This type of response is somewhere between a rejection and an acceptance, because it demands more work and resubmission from you yet makes no promises.

For example, I received a letter from an editor regarding a story picture book I'd submitted. She felt it had promise but wanted it totally rewritten from a different point of view. Then, she said, she would be willing to take another look at it.

If you get this type of response, it is up to you to decide, first, whether you agree with the editor that your story might work well from a different viewpoint and, second, if you're willing to do the rewriting without a firm promise of acceptance once you complete it.

Also in this response category is a note with the returned manuscript inviting you to submit the same manuscript at a later date. A couple years ago, I submitted an article on armadillos to a children's magazine. I received a nice note from the editor that they had "in the pipeline" a story with an armadillo as the main character. She invited me to wait 18 months and then resubmit the article. This still was not an acceptance—my decision at this point was whether I wanted to try a different market or hold off in the hope that this editor would accept the manuscript 18 months hence.

The "A" Word!

I imagine that most writers can tell you the exact details of that happy moment when they received their first contracts, no matter how small. I can't quite describe the feeling. I remember that my first response was to dance around the room chanting, "Thank you, Jesus!" In that moment, all my hard work, all my writing efforts seemed affirmed. I wanted to shout to the world, "I made it! I'm a writer!"

I must admit that at that time, I believed getting that first contract meant it would be easy-going from then on, that "accepts" would begin rolling in...not!

That, of course, is a humbling wake-up call, God's reminder that we can never take for granted the talents with which He's blessed us.

Even now, many years, many rejects, and a precious few dozen contracts later, I still praise God for every "accept" I receive.

Often, contracts are preceded by a "preliminary" acceptance letter. For example, I received a letter that began this way:

Chapter 11: Wait on Publishers

I am pleased to inform you that we are interested in publishing (name of manuscript) as part of our Animal Friends Series. We feel that it will really speak to the heart of young Christians. As you know, this would be a work-for-hire assignment, offering a flat fee of (amount), payable on receipt of the finalized manuscript. If these terms are acceptable to you, please let me know by (date) and I will forward a contract to you...

Publishing contracts are often written in "legalize"; unless you are able to translate and understand all the "hereinafter known as..." and "pursuant to..." clauses, consider having an attorney friend go over the contract for you. I am fortunate to have such a friend within my faith community who does this for me.

These contracts, whether for magazine or book manuscripts, cover such things as rights, advances, royalties, foreign/electronic sales, reprints, and legal responsibilities (for example, if someone you mention in your book sues for slander, who is responsible, you, the publisher, or both?). Know what you're signing.

Faith Statements

In the Christian publishing market, you will occasionally have a contract or publishing agreement that is accompanied by a faith statement that you must sign in addition to the contract or agreement in order to complete the publishing terms. These specify, usually in list form, the creed/beliefs in detail of the publication and denomination it represents. Read these carefully to be sure that you do agree with everything contained in that statement.

For example, one of my colleagues received such as a faith statement that included the belief that the Pope is the Antichrist. She is not Catholic but she still did not agree with this statement and, as much as she hated to turn down a contract, she had the integrity to not sign a document that was contrary to her beliefs.

Negotiations?

You certainly have the right to try to negotiate any of the terms of the contract with which you are not satisfied. Obviously, this is done before you sign the contract.

Be very specific about what terms you wish to negotiate and what adjustments would be acceptable to you.

Of course, you run the risk of having the publisher refuse to negotiate; then you must decide your next step. Is it worth sticking to your guns and thereby losing the contract?

Prayerfully weigh your options.

If you are fortunate enough to have an agent, your agent would be the intermediary between you and your prospective publisher.

Chapter 11: *Wait on Publishers*

Signed and Sealed—Time to Deliver

Your contract will have spelled out terms of rewriting and revisions and, most likely, a timetable for you to deliver any rewrites ascribed to you.

An editor will be assigned to work with you. Develop a good relationship with him or her. If the editor is making the bulk of the changes, he or she will share those with you. Be flexible on your approval—or not—of the changes the editor has made or requests you to make. Remember that the editor's goal is the same as yours: to produce the best story, article, or book you can, which is in both your best interests.

Illustrations/Covers

Illustrations and artwork to accompany fiction and nonfiction magazine submissions accepted for publication are almost always done by the publisher's art department.

If you are supplying photographs as illustrations, your payment for these should be part of your contract.

If you have signed a book contract and your book requires illustrations, and if you are not an illustrator (my illustrations would be stick people!), the publisher will select an illustrator for your book. You *can* recommend a friend or colleague to the publisher, but as a rule, publishers have a "stable" of artists that they prefer using.

Generally speaking, the illustrator reports to the publisher, not to you. Here again, let the illustrator use his or her God-given talents. Publishers use their vast experience in choosing the illustrators whose work they believe best match writers' styles. If your book requires only a cover illustration, an illustrator or the publisher's art department will design that for you.

Marketing/Promotion

Depending on the type of publisher you use, none, some, or all of the marketing might fall on your shoulders. This is another aspect of publishing that is spelled out in the contract.

Your editor might ask for your ideas to help promote the book, such as your suggesting a well-respected professional or clergy member who might be willing to write a foreword to your book. Be open to supplying any hints or information you can; again, it is in both your best interests to sell your book!

Also be open to making school visits, taking part in book signings, and "talking up" your book at church or at any gatherings in which you take part.

Chapter 11: *Wait on Publishers*

Let your local Christian bookstores know that you have a book coming out and are available for signings and/or readings.

Do you have a church festival? Offer to sign and sell your books and give a percentage of sales to the church.

If your local newspaper has a book reviewer, send him or her a copy of your book and request a review.

Start Your Publications Résumé

Even before that magazine story or article or book is published and in your hands, begin your publications list or résumé. There is nothing more affirming or uplifting. Head it however you like (mine has contact information, much like a regular résumé, and then in all caps and centered, the heading PUBLICATIONS LISTING), and then make two subheadings and make your first entry (I'm "inventing" the magazine title):

<u>Periodicals</u>
"Playing Soccer with Jesus," in *Christian Kids Alive!*, forthcoming fall 2011.

<u>Books</u>

It took a while before I had anything under the "books" subheading. Still, making that first entry in my publications list made me feel like a real writer, a working writer—at last! It also served as motivation for me to begin new projects and get them on the market. I hope it will serve the same purpose for you.

Writing Exercise

Draft a status query letter that you can use as a template when it comes time to check on past due manuscripts. Remember to be polite and concise.

...your faith should not stand in the wisdom of men, but in the power of God.

—1 Cor. 2:5

Chapter 12
Giving Back

Framed and hanging above my computer is this quote from the late, great writer and inspirational speaker, Leo Buscaglia: "The fact that I can plant a seed and it becomes a flower, share a bit of knowledge and it becomes another's, smile at someone and receive a smile in return, are to me continual spiritual exercises."

I'd never heard of Mr. Buscaglia until 1982, when I listened to his children's book, *The Fall of Freddie the Leaf*, being read on public television. In the gentlest, most beautiful language imaginable, he explained the cycle of life to young readers.

It was at this time that I began to wonder if I might someday hone my writing talents toward the high calling of writing children's literature. I still have my copy of *The Fall of Freddie the Leaf*, which I re-read often, savoring every word.

Buscaglia had another saying that has lived on since his untimely death in 1998: "We should determine to live for something. May I suggest that it be creating joy for others, sharing what we have for the betterment of personkind, bringing hope to the lost and love to the lonely. Only you will be able to discover, realize, develop and actualize your uniqueness. And when you do, it's your duty to then 'give it away.'"

Why Give It Away? (at Least Some of It)

In my opinion, we writers of Christian children's literature share our joy and our faith with every word we write. That is our primary mission.

But, we do need to eat and pay rent or mortgages, and we need to get paid, "...for the labourer is worthy of his hire" (Luke 10:7). Scripture also enjoins us to share our God-given talents: "As every man hath received the gift, even so minister the same one to another, as good stewards of the manifold grace of God" (1 Peter 4:10).

Those of us who are regular tithers do give back some of our writing income, but not all giving is monetary.

Chapter 12: *Giving Back*

How Can I Gift My Writing?

If you have been studying the Christian children's publishing market, you've discovered two things regarding how much money you might earn when writing for it: first, the payment rate is lower for writers than in many secular markets; and, second, there are several publishers—particularly of magazines—which do not pay other than in contributor copies and, in some cases, a subscription to that publication. Contributing to nonpaying markets is certainly one way of giving back by sharing your talent. Here are a few more suggestions, right in your own faith community.

Design a Children's Page for Your Church Newsletter

Volunteer to create such a page and to write/design it for each issue. These can contain Scripture, prayers, puzzles, quizzes—look at samples from other church newsletters that contain children's pages.

Volunteer as "Public Relations Writer" for Your Youth Director/Pastor

You may be surprised how much "stuff" needs to be written, everything from letters and forms for parents to announcements for the church bulletin to news releases.

Become a Volunteer "Parish/Church Reporter"

If you are a member of a denominational church, chances are there is a regional or national publication, often a newspaper or journal, to which news releases about activities at your church can be submitted. For example, in Texas, *The Baptist Standard* publishes such articles for all Baptist churches in the state.

Obituary Writer

I know, I know, this doesn't exactly sound inviting; however, consider this—not everyone is a writer, and when a loved one dies, there may be no one in the family who feels able to write an obituary.

I never thought about this until our church secretary called a couple years ago. She knew that I write, and asked me to write an obituary for a recent widow who had no one left in her family and who had no idea how to write her husband's obit. Interviewing her and getting the information I needed was a release for her and an emotional experience for me.

If this loving way to give back interests you, let your pastor or church office know that

Chapter 12: *Giving Back*

you are volunteering to write obituaries for those in need of this service.

Helping Seniors

Due to such conditions as failing vision and short-term memory issues, many seniors are in need of someone to write letters for them for insurance and other business matters. You can volunteer to help!

We had one poor soul in my faith community who was the victim of identity theft and needed letters written to the creditors who were mercilessly hounding her.

Again, if you are interested in giving back in this way, let your church office staff know of your availability.

Start and Facilitate a Christian Children's Writers' Group

If you've been writing for some time, you may already belong to a local writers' group or chapter of a national writers' organization, such as those referenced in Appendix B.

But beginning a subgroup within an existing organization or a separate group just for those who want to minister to children through their writing is certainly worthy of consideration.

Assess the interest level for such a venture by putting out feelers via "free" publicity sources such as your local Christian bookstores, coffee houses, church newsletters, and the bulletin board in your local supermarket.

If you find there is enough interest to start a small group (small is better!), offer to host an informational session at your home.

As with any writers' group, support and critiques are often the main activities, although how your group will function and what its mission will be should be a group decision and the focus of your first meeting.

I'm sure you can think of other ways in which you can share your writing talent in celebration of this special gift from God. If you're blessed not only with writing talent but also with computer know-how, perhaps you can design, edit, and/or maintain your church Website.

I handle all the publicity for the ladies' organization at my church.

In the past, I've also mentored children, particularly those needing help writing a coherent essay.

Pray for guidance and listen for an answer; the Lord will lead you to just the right opportunities to give away some of your writing talent.

Chapter 12: *Giving Back*

Go Forth and Sow Seeds

I'm so glad you took the time to read this book. I hope that in so doing, you've become excited about launching your own ministry of writing in one or more of the many genres of literature for Christian children.

I can't guarantee that you'll become wealthy, but I can guarantee you a storehouse of riches of the heart as you sow seeds in young Christians. "...the seed in the good soil, these are the ones who have heard the word in an honest and good heart, and hold it fast, and bear fruit with perseverance." (Luke 8:15, NASB)

I'll be looking for your byline on magazine stories and articles, as well as on books at my local Christian bookstore.

Writing Exercise

Write a paragraph about the way(s) you already give back or plan to give back/give away your writing talent.

Appendix A
Reference Resources for Christian Children's Writers

Essential Resources

Bible

Dictionary

English usage/grammar book, such as *Merriam Webster's Guide to English Usage*

Thesaurus

The Christian Writer's Manual of Style, Robert Hudson, editor. Grand Rapids, Michigan: Zondervan, 2004.

Christian Writers' Market Guide (published annually), Sally E. Stuart. Carol Stream, Illinois: Tyndale House Publishing.

Recommended Resources

Author Law A to Z: A Desktop Guide to Writers' Rights and Responsibilities, Sallie

Randolph, Stacy Davis, Anthony Elia, and Karen Dustman. Capital Ideas, 2005.

The Complete Idiot's Guide to Writing Christian Fiction, Ron Benrey. New York, NY: Alpha (Penguin Books), 2007.

For the Write Reasons: 31 Writers, Agents, and Editors Share Their Experience with Christian Publishing, Marybeth Whalen, Editor. Winepress Publishing, 2005.

The Little Handbook to Perfecting the Art of Christian Writing: Getting Your Foot in the Door, Leonard Goss and Don Aycock. Nashville, Tennessee: B & H Books, 2006.

Where to Find It in the Bible: The Ultimate A to Z Resource, Ken Anderson. Thomas Nelson Publishers, 2004.

Write His Answer: A Bible Study for Writers, 2nd Ed., Mary Bagnull. ACW Press, 2001.

Appendix B
Professional and Educational Resources for Christian Writers of Children's Literature

Education

If you feel the need to brush up on writing basics in general or would like to take a course in writing for children, the following lists just a few of the many correspondence and/or online course offerings.

Your local community education program may also offer in-class courses at high schools—often these are in the evenings.

- Christian Writers Guild (ChristianWritersGuild.com)

- The Crafty Writer (theCraftyWriter.com)

- Institute of Children's Literature (institutechildrenslit.com)

- Writers College (writerscollege.com)

Professional Journals

While there is no magazine (of which I am aware) that focuses strictly on writing for children, the following are the main journals for writers, and often these contain articles on writing for children. All four of these are sold in chain bookstores, where you can browse copies before subscribing.

- *Poets & Writers Magazine*
- *The Writer*
- *Writer's Digest*
- *Writers' Journal*

Professional Organizations

The following are organizations that may be of interest to writers for Christian children. Visit their Websites for more specific information.

- American Christian Fiction Writers (acfw.com)

- American Christian Writers (membership includes their magazine) (acwriters.com)

Appendix B: *Professional and Educaational Resources*

- Jerry B. Jenkins Christian Writers Guild (christianwritersguild.com)

- Society of Children's Book Writers and Illustrators (scbwi.org)

Websites

There are oodles of Websites of interest to those of us who minister to Christian children through their writing. The ones I most often frequent are:

- FaithWriters.com
- KidMagWriters.com
- SermonSearch.com
- SpiritLedWriter.com
- Write4Kids.com

Appendix C
Recommended Reading by Age Group

Preschool

All Things Bright & Beautiful: A Collection of Prayer & Verse (Helen Lanzrein, Tiger Tails, 2007).

Creation—Touch and Feel (Heather Henning, Concordia, 2007).

God Made Spring: A Really Woolly & Friends Fuzzy, Shiny Flap Book (Thomas Nelson, Thomas Nelson Publishing, 2008).

God Made Wonderful Me (Genny Monchamp, Pauline Books & Media, 2008).

Love Your Neighbor (Cindy Kenney, ZonderKidz, 2004).

My ABC Bible Verses: Hiding God's Word in Little Hearts (Susan Hunt, Yvette Banek, Illus., Crossway Books & Bibles, 1998).

My Big Birthday: A Carry Me Along Board Book (Dandi Daley Mackall, ZonderKidz, 2005).

My Sing Along Bible (ZonderKidz, 2009).

The One Year Book of Devotions for Preschoolers (Crystal Bowman, Tyndale, 2009).

Who Is Coming to Our House? (Joseph Slate, Ashley Wolff, Illus., Putnam Juvenile, 2001).

Primary

Adopted and Loved Forever, 2nd Edition (Annetta E. Dellinger, Concordia, 2008).

The Beginner's Bible (Kelly Pulley, Illus., ZonderKidz, 2005).

Bible Story Hidden Pictures (Warner Press, 2006—activity book).

Get Me to the Ark on Time (Cuyler Black, Zondervan, 2010).

Jesus Wants All of Me, Prayer Edition (Phil A. Smouse, Barbour Publishing, 2007).

Let There Be Llamas (Virginia Kroll, Pauline Books & Media, 2006).

Appendix C: *Recommended Reading by Age Group*

Let's Go on a Mommy Date (Karen Kingsbury, Dan Andreasen, ZonderKidz, 2008).

Mary's First Thanksgiving: An Inspirational Story of Gratefulness (Kathy-jo Wargin and Robert Papp, Illus., ZonderKidz, 2008).

Mission Possible: A 40-day Adventure with Jesus (Charles R. Swindoll, Thomas Nelson, 2009).

What Happens When Children Pray: Learning to Talk and Listen to God (Evelyn Christenson, Liz Duckworth, and Joy Dunn Keenan, Chariot Victor Publishing, 1997).

Intermediate

Canaan's Land (John Evans, Create Space, 2008).

The Case for Christ for Kids (Lee Strobel, Zondervan, 2010).

Coming Home (Max Lucado, Crossway Books & Bibles, 2007).

Faithgirlz: Girls Rock! Devotions for You (Kristi Holl, ZonderKidz, 2005).

A Girl after God's Own Heart: A Tween Adventure with God (Elizabeth George, Harvest House, 2010).

A House Divided—Willie Plummet (Paul Buchanan and Rod Randall, Concordia, 2001).

Little Visits with God, 4th Edition (Martin Simon, Concordia, 2006).

Now You're Cooking: Ten Short Stories with Recipes (Diana R. Jenkins and Diane M. Lynch, Pauline Books & Media, 2009).

The One Year Devotions for Boys (Debbie Bible and Betty Free, Editors, Tyndale Kids, 2000).

Star of Light (Patricia St. John, Moody Publishers, 2002).

Teens/Young Adults

Chosen! Won! Devotions for Teens by Teens (Concordia, 2007).

Drawing Marissa (Jessica Adriel, Little Lauren Books, 2008).

Appendix C: *Recommended Reading by Age Group*

Final Touch (Brandi Lynn and Amberly Collins, Zondervan, 2010).

God's Little Instruction Book for Teens (David C. Cook, David C. Cook Publishing, 2003).

Growing Up Christian: Have You Taken Over Ownership of Your Relationship with God? (Karl Graustein and Mark Jacobsen, P & R Publishing, 2005).

A Guy's Guide to Life: How to Become a Man in 224 Pages or Less (Jason Boyett, Thomas Nelson, 1992).

How to Stay Christian in College (J. Budziszewski, NAV Press, 2004).

I Am Not Ashamed: 50 Devotions for Teens on Romans (Laurie Polich, Abingdon Press, 2003).

Jesus Speaks to Teens (Vicki J. Kuyper, Bethany House, 2004).

Lies Young Women Believe: And the Truth that Sets Them Free (Nancy Leigh DeMoss and Dannah Gresh, Moody Publishing, 2008).

Bibliography

Chapter 1

Hample, Stuart and Eric Marshall. *Children's Letters to God*. New York: Workman Publishing Group, 1991.

Gorky, Maxim. "Famous Maxim Gorky Quotations." Quotes.net/quote/7896.

Bryson, Judy. "The States of Spiritual Growth," *Christianity Today*. Christianitytoday.com/childrensministry/pioneerclubs/stagesofspiritualgrowth.html.

Frost, Robert. "The Road Not Taken," publicdomainpoems.com/robertfrost.html.

Chapter 2

"*Pockets* Writer's Guidelines." pockets.upperroom.org/writers-guidelines/.

"Writer's Guidelines: Children's Books," Pauline Kids. pauline.org/WritersGuidelinesChildrensBooks/tabid/247/Default.aspx.

Chapter 3

Alcott, Louisa May. *Little Women*. New York: Signet Classics, 1983.

Angelettie, Lisa. "Article Writing: How to Create an Ideal Writing Workspace." lisaangelettieblog.com/article-writing-how-to-create-an-ideal-writing-workspace/.

Andersen, Ken. *Where to Find It in the Bible: The Ultimate A to Z Resource.* Nashville: Thomas Nelson Publishers, 2004 (original copyright 1997).

Myers, Bill. "Frequently Asked Questions," home page. Billmyers.com.

Chapter 4

Masthead, *Bread for God's Children*. Arcadia, Florida. (Website: breadministries.com.).

Masthead, *SHINE brightly*. Grand Rapids, Michigan. (Website: gemsgc.org.).

Chapter 5

Muldoon, Kathleen. "The Truth of the Matter," *Bread for God's Children*, Issue 2, 2006.

Robert, Yvonne. "How to Write A Christian Stage Play." eHow.com

Chapter 6

Adair, Amy. "Are You Living Your Faith?" *Ignite Your Faith*, Fall, 2008.

Chapter 7

Milton, John."Areopagitica, A Speech for the Liberty of Unlicensed Printing," speech delivered to Parliament of

England in 1644; transcript in *Today in Literature*, todayinliterature.com.

Muldoon, Kathleen. *Yes I Can! A Kid's Guide to Dealing with Physical Challenges,* St. Meinrad, IN: Abbey Press, 2010.

Subject Guide to Children's Books in Print, R.R. Bowker, LLC (published annually—they also publish *Children's Books in Print*, which is arranged by title and author.

www.christianbooks.com. This website is the online resource for Christian Book Distributors. It is the Christian equivalent of Amazon.com.

Chapter 8

"Manuscript Guidelines," Ambassador Books. ambassadorbooks.com/guidelines.asp.

Christian Booksellers Association (CBA), cbaonline.org.

Underdown, Harold D. "Writing and Publishing Board Books," underdown.org/board-books.htm.

Giblin, James Cross. *The Giblin Guide to Writing Children's Books*, CT: Writer's Institute Publications, 2005.

Malzeke. "How to Create a Book Dummy for Your Children's Picture Book Story,"ehow.com/how_4504619_dummy-childrens-picture-book-story.html.

Forster, E.M. *Aspects of the Novel*, Orlando: Mariner Books, 1956.

Taormina, Agatha. "Novels," nvcc.edu/home/ataormina/novels.

Chapter 10

Children's Book Council, FAQ. Answers.yahoo.com/questions/index. "Do I need to copyright my manuscript before contacting an agent?"

Chapter 12

Short, Steven. "The World of Leo Buscaglia," in *How to Get a Life, Volume 1: Empowering Wisdom for the Heart and Soul,* Lawrence Baines and Daniel McBrayer, Editors, Humanics Trade Group, 2003.

Index

Activities, 100, 101, 143
Activity books, 143, 216
Adventures. See Fiction, Adventures.
Age targeting, 12, 18-28, 58, 74-77, 88, 104, 112, 116, 123-136, 139, 143, 148, 149, 151, 155, 161, 165
Agents, 36, 115, 178-179, 196, 210, 224
Anderson, Ken, 49, 159, 210
Anecdotes, 91, 103, 149
Artwork, 128, 146, 197-198
Audience, 17-28
Beginner readers, 21-23, 75, 129-130, 144
Beginnings, 71-72, 91, 127, 135, 175
Bible stories, 31-32, 57, 66, 148, 216
 Embellished, 121-122
 Retold, 21, 77-78, 121-122, 126
Bible studies, 144-146
Bible versions, 48-49, 146
Biblical principles, 119, 127
Bibliographies, 94-95, 172,
Biographies, 57, 86-87, 89-90, 93, 146-147,

Biographies (cont'd), 175
Board books, 20, 31-32, 36, 107, 112, 121, 123-125, 126, 148, 150, 153-154, 215, 223
Bowman, Crystal, 3, 7, 105, 216
Bryson, Judy, 19, 21, 22, 25, 221
Buscaglia, Leo, 201-202, 224
Chapter books, 36, 130-132, 173
Characters, 65, 66, 68, 69, 71, 72, 77, 78, 116, 117, 119, 121, 129, 131, 132, 133, 134, 135, 154, 160
Christensen, Evelyn, 97-99
Christian living, 148-149
Christian perspective, 85-89
Christian values, 14, 118, 122, 148-149
Church history, 150-153
Columns/Departments, 101-102
Concept books, 153-154
Conflict, 70-73, 120
Contemporary stories, 39, 70, 120-121, 122, 131-132, 146-147, 173, 176, 185
Contracts, 127, 137, 141, 147, 178, 182, 184, 188, 194-198
Copyrighting, 177-178, 224

Cover letters, 102, 169-171, 172, 175, 192
Crafts, 34, 57, 64, 96-97, 101, 154-155
Denominations, 22, 24-25, 34, 35, 57, 59, 62, 76, 102, 168, 175, 196, 204
Departments. *See* Columns/Departments.
Devotions, 34, 57, 84, 100, 155-157, 158, 159, 216, 217, 218, 219
Dialogue, 40, 66, 68, 76, 77, 78, 110, 121, 147, 151, 172
Drama, 78-79, 157
Electronic books (ebooks/e-books), 46, 182
Endings, 73-74, 91-92, 127, 135, 175
Evans, John, 5, 7, 181-184, 217
Faith element, 14, 68, 80-81, 120, 126, 136
Faith journeys, 13, 26, 56, 87, 100, 111-113, 134
Faith testimonies, 57
Fantasy. *See* Fiction, Fantasy.
Feature articles, 32, 38, 57
Fiction
  Adventures, 75, 116-117, 134, 217, 218
  Historical, 117-118, 135
  Fantasy, 76, 117
  Mystery, 119-120

Fiction (cont'd),
  Romance, 122
  Science Fiction, 115, 117
  Sports, 122-123
  Suspense, 119-120
Fictionalization, 77
Fillers, 102-103
Games, 57, 84, 97-101, 161
Giblin, James Cross, 124, 223
Gifting writing talent, 203-206
Grammar, 15, 40, 48, 176, 209
Guidelines, 18, 29, 30, 33-42, 87-88, 116, 150, 167, 168, 172, 173, 179, 185, 191, 192, 221, 223
Historical Fiction. *See* Fiction, Historical
History, 157-159
Hudson, Robert, 48, 209
Humor, 40, 57, 118, 130
Ideas, 31, 52, 87, 101, 105, 107-111, 138, 154, 177-178
Illustrations, 120, 125-127, 159, 197-198
Illustrator, 127-128, 159, 197-198, 213
Intermediate readers, 23-25, 98, 117, 139
Internet, 48, 93, 139, 140
Interviews, 86, 92, 93-94, 95, 204
Journals, 110, 156, 158-159, 212
Louis, Jo, 7, 134
Magazines, Themed, 35, 38, 59, 171

Index

Manuscript submissions, *See* Submissions, Manuscript
Market analysis, 37-42
Markets, 29-42
Martin, Etta G., 5, 7, 68, 87
Masthead, 38, 60, 62
Meditations, 155-157
Middle, 72-73, 91, 127, 135, 175
Middle grade readers, 23-25, 75, 96, 98, 117, 118, 119, 132, 134, 135, 138, 151, 158, 160
Mission, 13, 15, 34, 57, 60, 86, 116, 172, 202, 206
Moral message, 39, 59, 67
Multicultural, 35, 116, 119
Myers, Bill, 52, 222
Mystery. *See* Fiction, Mystery
Negotiations, 196
Nonfiction, 83-104, 109, 110, 113, 134, 136, 137-165, 175, 176, 197
Novel, 63, 107, 132-136, 138, 223, 224
Openings, *See* Beginnings
Outlines, 112, 136, 138, 140, 172-173, 176-177, 185
Payment, 61-62, 195, 197, 203
Permissions, 94, 95, 157, 161

Photographs, 95, 147, 197
Picture books, 11, 105, 108, 119, 120, 121, 124, 126-128, 130, 140, 141, 146, 152, 157, 159, 162, 168, 223
Plot, 39, 40, 49, 51, 59, 66, 68-69, 71, 77, 81, 118, 120, 121, 122, 127, 129-136, 138, 175
POD, *See* Print-on-demand
Poetry, 57, 97, 148, 160
Pray, 23, 24, 75, 92, 107, 162, 206, 217
Prayers, 24, 30, 51-53, 83, 84, 100, 101, 112, 117, 130, 148, 156, 160-161, 162, 164, 167, 174, 187, 192, 196, 203, 215, 216
Preschoolers, 19-21, 31, 57, 66, 75, 79, 96, 97, 98, 118, 120, 121, 143, 153, 160, 215-216
Primary readers, 21-23, 75, 96, 98, 110, 111, 119, 143, 145, 151, 160, 216-217
Primary sources. *See* Sources, Primary.
Print-on-demand, 182-184
Profiles, 57, 86-87, 92
Promotion, 184, 198-199
Proposals, 102, 137, 138, 175
Publisher responses, 168, 187-197
Puppet shows, 78-79
Puzzles, 57, 84, 97-100, 161, 203
Query, 140, 141, 151, 171-177, 185, 187-

Query (cont'd), 189, 200
Quizzes, 31, 57, 64, 97-99, 203
Readability, 40
Rebuses, 57, 79-80
Recipes, 57, 96-97, 101, 218
Rejects, 40, 68, 160, 168, 188-194
Research, 39, 58, 82, 92-94, 103, 108, 135, 138, 140, 147, 151, 153, 158, 165, 175, 181
Resources, 209-224
Résumés, 199-200
Robert, Yvonne, 78, 222
Romance. See Fiction, Romance
S.A.S.E., 167-168, 172, 177, 179, 188
Sample copies, 33, 34, 38, 58, 184, 203
Schedule, 49-51
Science Fiction. See Fiction, Science Fiction
Scripture, 23, 39, 40, 48, 49, 57, 60, 68, 76, 77, 78, 86, 96, 100, 102, 134, 144-146, 149, 151, 153, 155, 156, 157, 158, 202, 203
Self-help books, 162
Self-publishing, 16, 180-185
Setting, 65, 66, 70-71, 117, 119
Short stories, 65-81, 218
Skits, 57, 78-79, 157
Sources, Primary, 93

Sports Fiction. See Fiction, Sports Fiction.
Story picture books, 126, 128, 157, 174, 193
Stuart, Sally E., 11-12, 36-37, 48, 102, 179, 209
Style, 15, 31-32, 42, 47, 48, 58, 112, 139, 142, 145, 147, 149, 154, 176, 198, 209
Subheadings, 91, 199, 200
Submissions,
  Electronic, 46, 169, 188
  Manuscript, 34, 35, 36, 59, 97, 113, 169-171, 177, 185, 188
Summaries, 81, 91, 104, 113, 140, 165, 175-176
Suspense. See Fiction, Suspense.
Taormina, Agatha, 133, 224
Teens, 13, 15, 25-26, 27, 31, 32, 36, 56, 76-77, 90, 91, 96, 98, 99, 104, 109, 120, 122, 132, 134, 139, 144, 148, 149, 155, 158, 159, 162, 163, 164, 175, 218-219
Theme, 69, 75, 81, 87, 88, 101, 108, 111, 120, 122, 135, 139, 143, 154, 168, 170, 171, 177, 191, 192
Themed magazines. See Magazines, Themed
Theology, 150-153
Timeline, 70, 75, 135, 158
Tone, 32, 39, 40, 42, 58, 142
Tracking systems, 179-180

Index

Tweens, 23-25
Underdown, Harold, 123-124, 223
Voice, 58, 147, 158
Woller, Judy, 7, 103
Workspace, 15, 43-49, 222
Writing ministry, 7, 13, 14, 15, 18, 33, 52, 62, 80, 97, 104, 105, 106, 163, 207
Young adults, *See* Teens

About the Author

Kathleen Muldoon is a retired journalist and current writing instructor for the Institute of Children's Literature.

She has authored sixteen children's books, nonfiction and fiction, in the educational and Christian markets, as well as contributed stories to children's book anthologies.

Her stories have appeared in such magazines as *Bread for God's Children, My Friend, My Light, Primary Treasure, On the Line*, and *Primary Days*. She also writes a bimonthly column, "Kids in Action," for *Action*, a national publication of United Spinal Association.

When not writing for children, she enjoys teaching writing workshops and adult continuing education courses, as well as writing stories and articles for adult inspirational publications such as the *Chicken Soup for the Soul* books and *Guideposts*.

www.ingramcontent.com/pod-product-compliance
Lightning Source LLC
Chambersburg PA
CBHW050632300426
44112CB00012B/1760